BANK STREET COLLEGE OF EDUCATION

# THE BEST
# CHILDREN'S
# BOOKS
# OF THE YEAR

## 100TH ANNIVERSARY EDITION

SELECTED BY THE

### CHILDREN'S BOOK COMMITTEE

THE CHILDREN'S BOOK COMMITTEE IS AN AFFILIATE OF
THE BANK STREET CENTER FOR CHILDREN'S LITERATURE

FOREWORD BY JON SCIESZKA

TEACHERS COLLEGE • COLUMBIA UNIVERSITY
NEW YORK AND LONDON

# CONTENTS

# FOREWORD

If there were a riddle about the volume you are holding in your hands, it might go something like: What is gold, one hundred years old, but also brand new?

It's one hundred years old because that's how long Bank Street has been selecting *The Best Children's Books of the Year.* It's brand new because this is the first year that Teachers College Press is taking on the publishing and distribution. And it is gold because this collection is the gold standard of quality literature for children.

Bank Street has always championed good literature as the foundation of literacy, learning, and development at all levels of childhood education. Now they are joining with Teachers College Press to get their good work out to as many readers as possible. And boy do we need it.

As the first Ambassador for Young People's Literature, I have been given a Library of Congress medal, a really long title, and the mission to promote the best in children's books. I love the Children's Book Committee at Bank Street College of Education because they make my job so much easier. Watch how:

Looking for a good book to get a child you know interested in reading?

Read this.

Done. Wasn't that nice of them? Thanks, Bank Street and Teachers College Press.

I could go on about the hundreds of great titles carefully chosen by a group of very smart and dedicated people, the perfect and perfectly practical Tips for Parents, the incredibly useful organization by age and interest. But that's all pretty obvious. And it's all in the book.

So thanks and congratulations all around. Thanks for making my Ambassador job easy. Congratulations on helping us answer the riddle: How do you get a child reading?

The Bank Street *Best Children's Books of the Year.*

Ambassador Jon Scieszka
Brooklyn, NY

# ABOUT THE
# CHILDREN'S BOOK COMMITTEE

## History of the Children's Book Committee

As we celebrate our 100th year, we'd like to offer readers a brief history of our Committee. We began in 1909 as part of the family life education program of the Child Study Association of America, an organization devoted to guiding parents in their understanding of child development.

At the time, a nascent "parent education" movement fostered a growing awareness of the emotional needs of children, and of how books might affect children's feelings of themselves and the world around them. As "expert" opinions of psychiatrists, psychologists, and educators filtered down to parents, the Child Study Association decided to evaluate current literature for children, and to prepare and publish booklists to guide parents, librarians, and teachers in the selection of developmentally appropriate reading materials. Interestingly enough, the Committee decided right from the start to publish only *positive* reviews and recommendations.

Its first product was a modest pamphlet, but more ambitious lists soon followed. Eventually, with a rapidly expanding number of new children's books being published, the Committee adopted a more organized reviewing process, which continues to this day.

For many years the Committee's reviews appeared in the monthly (and later quarterly) magazine published by the Association. When the magazine was discontinued, the Committee compiled its own annual booklet, the "Children's Books of the Year," which has been published and distributed yearly since 1936.

The Committee eventually expanded its mandate in a number of significant ways. It collected and edited anthologies of children's stories and published specific lists in response to requests from parents, organizations, or specific needs that arose in the community. It also arranged lectures to promote public interest in children's literature and invited children to discuss their preferences in books, which eventually led to the inclusion of Young Reviewers on the Committee.

In addition, the Committee established an annual award in 1942 to encourage the writing and publishing of books "for children and young people dealing realistically with some of the problems in the world." The Committee now also bestows an annual award for the best poetry book for young readers as well as an award for a nonfiction book that "serves as an inspiration for young readers."

By 1977, the Child Study Association was forced to discontinue its programs because of financial difficulties, but the Children's Book Committee was invited to continue its groundbreaking work at the Bank Street College of Education, where it remains to this day. Here its outreach broadened, not only in increasing the circulation of its list, but in the wider range of its membership.

Today's Committee comprises some 35 members—all volunteers—from various professions and backgrounds concerned with children and books: writers, illustrators, editors, librarians, teachers, and parents. Members use their skills and expertise to foster the unique point of view bequeathed to us by our founding organization—namely, *how* books can affect young readers, and *what* books can do for *them*.

## *The 2009 Josette Frank Award*

*for*

### After Tupac & D Foster

by JACQUELINE WOODSON

published by G. P. Putnam's Sons

This award is given each year to honor a book or books of outstanding literary merit in which children or young people deal in a positive and realistic way with difficulties in their world and grow emotionally and morally. In addition to being a well-known author of articles about children's books, Josette Frank was the first editor of the Children's Book Committee publications and remained a member for over 60 years.

The prize to the author has been generously provided by The Florence L. Miller Memorial Fund.

## *The 2009 Claudia Lewis Award*

*for*

### The Surrender Tree:
### Poems of Cuba's Struggle for Freedom

by MARGUERITE ENGLE

published by Henry Holt Books for Young Readers

This award is given for the best poetry book of the year for young readers. A longtime member of the Committee, Claudia Lewis was an esteemed poet, author, and teacher of children's literature. She served on the faculty at Bank Street College of Education.

## *The 2009 Flora Stieglitz Straus Award*

*for*

### The Lincolns:
### A Scrapbook Look at Abraham and Mary

by CANDACE FLEMING

published by Schwartz and Wade

This award is given for a nonfiction book that serves as an inspiration to young readers. Flora Stieglitz Straus chaired the Children's Book Committee for over sixty years.

# How We Select Books

Of the 5,000 to 6,000 books the Children's Book Committee receives each year from publishers, only 650 end up on our list of best books. How are they selected? At weekly meetings, Committee members report on each book they have read and the book is discussed by the Committee as a whole. Every book is then given to a second member to read. Two members of the Committee must each consider a book "list worthy" for it to be accepted. If the first two readers disagree about a book, then a third reader evaluates it. Many books are also sent to Young Reviewers, 35 children between the ages of two and eighteen, who live throughout the U.S. The Young Reviewers program is unique to the Children's Book Committee and helps ensure that our adult perspective is also informed by children's own reactions and concerns.

But how does a Committee member decide that a book should be on the list? Whether it is a board book for toddlers, a picture book for young children, a novel for teens, or a factual account of a science topic or historical event, the book must be developmentally appropriate—suited to the cognitive, social, and emotional interests and needs of its intended audience. As educators we rely on academic theorists such as Piaget, Vygotsky, and Erickson, as well as our own extensive experience working with children, to inform us as to what content is developmentally appropriate. What is the cognitive development of the "typically developing" five-year-old? At what age is it appropriate to open a discussion of concentration camps? A useful thumbnail guide to child development is *Yardsticks: Children in the Classroom Ages 4–14* by Chip Wood (Northeast Foundation for Children, 3rd edition, 2007).

High literary quality is also an essential evaluative criterion. We want to endorse literature that contains rich, clear, well-crafted language; multidimensional characters; credible relationships, and interesting, creative plots. Similarly, illustrated books must exhibit artistic excellence, with pictures and text complementing one another; both elements, words, and images must be strong. Other criteria include positive treatment of ethnic, religious, social, and physical differences, and the absence of stereotypes. We are actively seeking books that not only reflect the diversity of children's own experiences but also prove to be a window into the wider world.

The information in nonfiction books must be accurate and presented clearly and engagingly, with maps, timelines, indexes, and diagrams included as called for to enhance content. Proper research methods, such as citation of sources and an inclusion of a bibliography, must also be evident. The nonfiction texts are fact-checked either by a Committee member's further research or the book is passed on to an expert in the field. We take advantage of Committee members' far-reaching social networks. It is not unusual for a reviewer to report back that a prominent historian, a biologist, a veterinarian, or an iron worker has an opinion about a book's content. We may give a book to the Bank Street College of Education School for Children psychologist for review or, when appropriate, ask a teacher to read aloud a book to her class.

We are often asked how differences of opinion are resolved. Each of us has his or her own process. Committee work hones our listening skills. Sometimes it is as simple as the presentation and acceptance of a picture book by the first reviewer. She might find that the plot and characters are age appropriate and, in her learned opinion, the title would be a delightful addition to books about going to school for a preschooler. Reviewer number two agrees that the illustrations are more than pleasing with their fabric collage style but that the rhyming text was forced in places. Given that there are so many "starting school" books, this title would not meet the criteria for inclusion in *The Best Children's Books of the Year*. Reviewer number one respectfully disagrees, perhaps reading aloud a portion of the text, perhaps pointing out that the unusual relationship between teacher and parent demonstrates its worthiness. The Chair of the Committee then asks for a third reviewer. The third reviewer may find merit in both sides and request a fourth. Committee members are ever aware of the finite length of the list and the volume of books published when advocating for a title. Rather than creating a tie-breaker, there is more of a consensus when finally deciding if a book should be listed.

A book that receives a star indicates that there was unanimous agreement that the book is not only one of the best books of the year, but also an outstanding title that would deserve a place in almost every school, public, or home library.

We value the opinions of our Young Reviewers. Two Committee members may be enthralled with a noted historian's densely written biography of an American Civil War soldier but might question its appeal to a young teen. The coordinators of the Young Reviewer program may indicate that they have the right fourteen-year-old for this book. We ask our Young Reviewers to rate the book, examine what makes this book special or different, and to react critically to its content. We ask, "Why do you think the author wrote this book? What do you think the author was trying to say?" A ten-year-old girl wrote about *Each Little Bird That Sings* by Deborah Wiles (Harcourt, 2005), "I think what Deborah was trying to say is that love is too strong to waste and to care for the ones you love. I think Deborah wrote this book because of something in her past and for her love of someone and because she wanted to tell everyone that there is hope."

When asked the question about *Lionel and the Book of Beasts,* by Edith Nesbit, retold by Michael Hague (HarperCollins, 2006), a five-year-old boy wrote, "He was trying to say that if people are scared they can learn how to be brave."

At the end of the year, the entire list is evaluated for diversity and balance of content in each category. During this final process, Committee members decide which books qualify as the very best to keep on the list.

## Tips For Parents

How do parents know which books are the best for their family out of the thousands of children's books published each year? We hope that this guide helps parents to select appropriate reading material for their children. Remember there is no one book for every child.

In her book *Reading Magic: Why Reading Aloud to Our Children Will Change Their Lives Forever* (Mariner Books, 2nd edition, 2008), celebrated author and educator Mem Fox declares that every child should have had read aloud to them 1,000 books by the time they enter preschool. This statement is not as outrageous as it seems. This reasonable goal can be accomplished by reading aloud three books a day. That's right, just three 32-page picture books each day. Each one takes only five to ten minutes to read aloud. We recommend that children hear an old favorite, one that Mom or Dad loves the best, and a new one. If you read aloud *I Stink* (McMullan, HarperCollins, 2006) three times in a row (there is no higher praise from a child than "Read it again!"), that counts. Reading aloud gives our children the gift of reading readiness, increased vocabulary, sequencing skills, listening skills, and comprehension. We suggest creating a reading time that is a predictable part of a child's daily schedule. If you are bored or your child's attention wanders, select another book or do something else.

What do we suggest that parents look for in books to read with their child?

- Is the book age appropriate?
- Does it contain rich language?
- For emergent readers, is there rhythm, rhyme, or repetition?
- Is it child-centric?
- Is there diversity of culture, not only reflecting the child's world but providing a window into others?

Here is a short developmental guide by age group to help you in selecting books for your children:

**Ages 0 to 2.5:** It is never too early to read aloud. Best for this age are board books such as *Gossie and Gertie* (Dunrea, HMC, 2002) and simple stories such as *Good Night Moon* (Brown, Harper, 1949).

**Ages 3 and up:** Concept books are books about numbers, letters, opposites, and colors. We love the primary colors and simple concepts of the *Maisy* books by Lucy Cousins (Candlewick, 2000). Parents can observe sophisticated design in *Growing Vegetable Soup* (Harcourt, 1987) by Lois Ehlert. The best also celebrate language, such as *Chicka Chicka Boom Boom* (Martin, S&S, 1989). This is the age that loves lift-the-flap books such as *Dear Zoo* (Campbell, MacMillan, 1982) and interactive stories such as *We're Going on a Bear Hunt* (Rosen, McElderry, 1989). Begin and end every day with a Mother Goose rhyme.

**Ages 4 and up:** Fours and fives love to tell and retell folktales such as *Goldilocks and the Three Bears* and *Anansi the Spider*. It is also time for classics such as *Whistle for Willie* (Keats, Viking, 1964), *The Tale of Peter Rabbit* (Potter, Warne, 1928), and of course books by Dr. Seuss such as *One fish, two fish, red fish, blue fish* (Random House Beginning Books, 1960). Children of this age like familiar characters: Ruby and Max, George and Martha, Clifford the Big Red Dog, and Curious George.

**Ages 5 and up:** At this age children show an interest in fairytales, folklore, and fables: a fascination with issues such as friendship, going to school, and monsters under the bed. They have a love of fact books and a great sense of humor; nothing is too silly. Author Judy Sierra is a favorite, from *Antarctic Antics* to *Tasty Baby Belly Buttons*. Choose poetry anthologies such as *Here's a Little Poem* by Jane Yolen (Candlewick, 2007) for reading aloud while sitting in a car or waiting in a doctor's office.

**Ages 6 and up:** Keep reading aloud longer picture books such as stories by Robert D. San Souci or biographies by Andrea Davis Pinkney, as well as starting on chapter books such as *Ramona the Pest* (Cleary, HarperCollins, 1968). At this age beginning readers are looking at *Biscuit* (Capucilli, HarperCollins, 1996) and confident readers are racing through early chapter books such as *Nate the Great* (Sharmat, Coward, McCann & Geoghegan, 1972) and *Henry and Mudge* (Rylant, Bradbury, 1987), elegantly illustrated picture books, and fact-filled illustrated nonfiction. Don't forget audio books, especially for car trips.

**Ages 7 and up:** We are entering the land of individual preferences. Try early chapter books such as *Gooney Bird Greene* (Lowry, HMC, 2002) and *Stink: The Incredible Shrinking Kid* (MacDonald, Candlewick, 2005). Children are selecting books by genre and series. They like school stories, myths, scary stories, ballet, and sports stories. Series include *Goosebumps, Baby-sitter's Club, A–Z Mysteries, The Zack Files,* and the adventures of Jack and Annie in *The Magic Tree House.*

**Ages 8, 9, 10:** We are firmly in the land of individual preferences. Look for books by genre, such as fantasy, science fiction, and mystery. Children are waiting anxiously for the next Percy Jackson or the new Kate DiCamillo.

**Ages 10 and up:** Parents need to continue to model reading. Are you helping children choose to read? Studies show a drop in independent reading for this age group. Provide a quiet time to read. Respect children's choices. You might not love graphic novels or comics, but they provide opportunities for increasing vocabulary and reading comprehension skills. On that note, why not try a few books in graphic format such as *Babymouse* (Holm, Random House, 2005) or *Satchel Paige: Striking Out Jim Crow* (Sturm, Jump at the Sun, 2007)? You may change your mind about literary quality.

**Ages 12 and up:** This is a time when children start pushing barriers and seeking peer approval. Competent readers can read anything, even adult books. Popular adult authors for teen readers include Octavia Butler, Stephen King, and Michael Crichton. High-interest areas include chick lit, science fiction, fantasy, history, horror, and adventure. Focused areas of nonfiction include math, history, and science.

**Ages 14 and up (High Schoolers):** Even though most teens are capable of reading almost anything for the purposes of this list, we select titles that were specifically published for teens. We are looking for high-interest fiction and nonfiction that specifically address teen issues such as human sexuality, social development, and relationships. It is even more important for this age group to have the freedom to self-select titles of their own interest because this is a skill that will serve them in their life-long learning.

Finally, self-selection is the key to instilling a love of books and reading. Surround your children with books. Make regularly scheduled trips to the public library. Children and teens need to practice making choices. If your child is in love with Spot, go there. If all she wants is books about dinosaurs or dogs, don't worry, this phase will pass. Or it won't, and she will become a paleontologist or a veterinarian. This guide provides a range of choices for every child. We wish you many hours of joyful browsing and reading.

## How To Use This Guide

Placing books in categories can prove to be a tricky endeavor. This guide is organized in as intuitive a way as possible, aiming to anticipate the needs of teachers, parents, grandparents, and other readers who are looking for that certain just-right book for a child at a certain age or consumed with a particular obsession. While many books could appear in multiple categories, we have tried to select the most appropriate one for each. We hope that the description provided for each selection makes all aspects of the book clear.

The first five sections of the booklist are devoted to fiction and are grouped by age: **Under Five, Five to Nine, Nine to Twelve, Twelve to Fourteen,** and, in a category new to the book this year, **Fourteen and Up**. Within each of these sections are topics such as "Adventure & Mystery," "Coming of Age," "Sports," and "Today." Some of the topics are common to every age group, some appear only in certain ones. For instance, "Beginning Readers" is found only in Five to Nine and "Folk & Fairy Tales" only in Five to Nine and Nine to Twelve.

Works of nonfiction—and other books that do not readily fit into the fiction category—are listed under **Special Interests**. Readers can find "Poetry" here, as well as a wide range of subject areas including "Ecology," "Health," "Math," and "Reference." Someone looking for a book filled with facts about insects, mummies, or ninjas, would likely find it in the Special Interests section.

Every section includes icons that help readers quickly identify certain types of books. For example, a ★ indicates a book of outstanding merit, a Ⓑ marks board books, and graphic novels are marked with a 📖. Each section shows the icons used in a key at its beginning. And every book description—a brief encapsulation of the story line, subject, or style of illustration—includes the age range deemed appropriate. A book might be listed in the Under Five section, but might appeal to readers aged four to six.

# UNDER FIVE

Marla Frazee 2008

 **★1, 2, Buckle My Shoe**
written and ill. by
Anna Grossnickle Hines
(Harcourt, $16.00) 978-0-15-206305-4
Dazzling fabric appliqués illustrate the traditional counting rhyme. (2–5)

## Arabella Miller's Tiny Caterpillar
written and ill. by Clare Jarrett
(Candlewick, $16.99) 978-0-7636-3660-9
Vibrant pencil and paper collages illustrate the life cycle of a caterpillar. (3–5)

## Bear Feels Scared
by Karma Wilson, ill. by Jane Chapman
(McElderry, $16.99) 978-0-689-85986-1
Big old Bear loses his way in the storm. Can his little friends save him? Evocative acrylics. (3–5)

 **The Big Bigger Biggest Book**
written and ill. by SAMi
(Chronicle, $14.95) 978-1-934706-39-8
Simple, bold, and bright illustrations explain comparisons in this appealing lift-the-flap book. (3–4)

## Big Little Monkey
by Carole Lexa Schaefer, ill. by Pierre Pratt
(Candlewick, $16.99) 978-0-7636-2006-6
Monkey sets out alone one morning to look for a playmate. Lush acrylic paintings. (4–6)

## A Birthday for Cow!
written and ill. by Jan Thomas
(Harcourt, $12.95) 978-0-15-206072-5
While pig and mouse make a wonderful surprise birthday cake for cow, duck knows what cow really would prefer. (3–5)

## A Child's Day: An Alphabet of Play
written and ill. by Ida Pearle
(Harcourt, $12.95) 978-0-15-206552-2
Act, blow, catch, dance—all the way to zoom. Playful cut-paper collages. (4–6)

## A Cold Winter's Good Knight
by Shelley Moore Thomas,
ill. by Jennifer Plecas
(Dutton, $15.99) 978-0-525-47964-2
Three boisterous young dragons promise to be good at the ball. Colorful ink and watercolor drawings capture the mischief. (4–6)

 **Dance with Me**
by Charles R. Smith Jr.,
ill. by Noah Z. Jones
(Candlewick, $8.99) 978-0-7636-2246-6
Rhymes and clear illustrations encourage the reader to move and sing along. (3–5)

---

## KEY

★ Outstanding merit

⧖ Babies & Toddlers

Ⓑ Board book

· **SERIES TITLE**
| (series books follow)

**(4-6)** Age range

---

## Danny's Drawing Book

written and ill. by Sue Heap
(Candlewick, $9.99) 978-0-7636-3654-8
A day at the zoo becomes an African adventure as a boy's imagination pulls us inside this book within a book. Pencil and bright acrylic art. (4–6)

## Dinosaur vs. Bedtime

written and ill. by Bob Shea
(Hyperion, $15.99) 978-142311335-5
A feisty dinosaur takes on a number of challenges, the most formidable of which is going to sleep. Bold, mixed-media illustrations (3–6)

## Dog and Bear: Two's Company

written and ill. by Laura Vaccaro Seeger
(Roaring Brook, $12.95) 978-1-59643-273-4
The special friendship between a dachshund and a stuffed bear is presented in three humorous stories. (3–5)

## ★Dog Day

by Sarah Hayes, ill. by Hannah Broadway
(FSG, $16.95) 978-0-374-31810-9
The first day of school is very successful when the new teacher turns out to be a dog. Funny, cheery illustrations. (4–7)

## The Doghouse

written and ill. by Jan Thomas
(Harcourt, $12.95) 978-0-15-206533-1
Mouse watches with alarm as each of his friends goes into the doghouse to retrieve a ball. Bright, bold illustrations. (4–6)

## ★Duck Dunks

by Lynne Berry, ill. by Hiroe Nakata
(Henry Holt, $16.95) 978-0-8050-8128-2
Count the five happy ducks as they enjoy a day at the beach. Lively watercolor and ink illustrations. (4–6)

## The Firefighters

by Sue Whiting, ill. by Donna Rawlins
(Candlewick, $15.99) 978-0-7636-4019-4
A clever weaving of fantasy play and real experience depicts the job of firefighters. Colorful acrylic illustrations. (4–7)

## Friends and Pals and Brothers, Too

by Sarah Wilson, ill. by Leo Landry
(Henry Holt, $16.95) 978-0-8050-7643-1
Two brothers enjoy the same things and are the best of friends. Enticing watercolors. (3–5)

## Grandma Calls Me Beautiful

by Barbara M. Joosse, ill. by Barbara Lavallee
(Chronicle, $16.99) 978-0-8118-5815-1
A Hawaiian grandmother's unconditional love for her granddaughter is captured in lyrical text and illustrations. (3–5)

## Granny's Dragon

by Lisa McCourt, ill. by Cyd Moore
(Dutton, $12.99) 978-0-525-47463-0
A youngster's bedtime monster fears are surmounted by her Granny's gentle but fearsome dragon. Bold, colorful illustrations. (3–5)

### • JUST LIKE US

## Ⓑ Having Fun! Together!

written and ill. by Jess Stockham
(Child's Play, $7.99) 978-1-84643-178-4, 978-1-84643-179-1
Fold-out flaps show similarities between the activities of baby animals and young children. Vivid, energetic illustrations. (1–3)

## Heart in the Pocket

by Laurence Bourguignon,
ill. by Valérie d'Heur
(Eerdmans, $16.50) 978-0-8028-5343-1
After numerous attempts, Mama Kangaroo finds a way to encourage her baby to leave the pouch. (3–5)

## Ⓑ I Like It When... / Me gusta cuando...

written and ill. by Mary Murphy,
trans. by F. Isabel Campoy and Alma Flor Ada
(Harcourt, $6.95) 978-0-15-206045-9
A look at the warm relationship between mother and child is presented with colorful illustrations. (3–6)

## I'm Bad!

by Kate McMullan, ill. by Jim McMullan
(HarperCollins, $16.99) 978-0-06-122971-8
Follow a romp through prehistoric land-
scapes with a cocky little dinosaur looking
for dinner. Bright, action-filled illustrations.
(4–7)

## In the Night Garden

by Barbara Joosse, ill. by Elizabeth Sayles
(Henry Holt, $16.95) 978-0-8050-6671-5
Three girls play in a garden before bedtime,
each imagining herself a different animal.
Poetic text, acrylic and pastel illustrations.
(4–6)

## It's Time to Sleep, My Love

by Eric Metaxas, ill. by Nancy Tillman
(Feiwel, $16.95) 978-0-312-38371-8
Lyrical rhymed text describes animal babies
settling down for the night. Beautifully
detailed digital and mixed-media illustrations. (3–5)

## Jack Wants a Snack

ill. by Pat Schories
(Front Street, $13.95) 978-1-59078-546-1
A puppy's quest to join a tea party will give
readers of this wordless book a giggle. (3–6)

## Jackson's Blanket

written and ill. by Nancy Cote
(Putnam, $16.99) 978-0-399-24694-4
A young boy, unwilling to give up his
beloved blanket, shares it with a newly
found pet. Gouache and watercolor illustrations. (3–6)

## A Kitten Tale

written and ill. by Eric Rohmann
(Knopf, $15.99) 978-0-517-70915-3
Three young kittens worry about the winter
snow, but the adventurous fourth kitten cannot wait. Simple text and bold, colorful illustrations. (3–5)

## Kitty Up!

by Elizabeth Wojtusik,
pictures by Sachiko Yoshikawa
(Dial, $12.99) 978-0-8037-3278-0
A kitten's adventure is portrayed with simple
rhyming words and bright, engaging illustrations. (1–3)

## The Little Bit Scary People

by Emily Jenkins, ill. by Alexandra Boiger
(Hyperion, $16.99) 978-142310075-1
A young girl observes that first impressions
can sometimes be misleading. Expressive
illustrations. (4–6)

## Little Blue Truck

by Alice Schertle, ill. by Jill McElmurry
(Harcourt, $16.00) 978-0-15-205661-2
A little truck moves a big dump truck with a
lot of help from friends. Rollicking, rhythmic
rhyming text and bright, gouache illustrations. (3–5)

## Little Boy

by Alison McGhee, ill. by Peter H. Reynolds
(Atheneum, $15.99) 978-1-4169-5872-7
The simple things that bring joy to a child's
daily life are rendered in ink and watercolors. (3–5)

## Little Rabbit's New Baby

written and ill. by Harry Horse
(Peachtree, $15.95) 978-1-56145-431-0
Brother rabbit is in for a surprise when he
tries to interact with his new baby triplet siblings. Delicate pen and ink and watercolor
illustrations. (3–5)

## The Little Yellow Leaf

written and ill. by Carin Berger
(Greenwillow, $16.99) 978-0-06-145223-9
An autumn leaf overcomes his fear of change
with the help of a friend. Elegant and clever
cut-paper illustrations. (3–6)

## ★Mail Harry to the Moon!

by Robie H. Harris, ill. by Michael Emberley
(Little, $16.99) 978-0-316-15376-8
Baby Harry's older brother wants his life
back the way it used to be. Humorous illustrations. (3–6)

## Marshmallow

written and ill. by Clare Turlay Newberry
(HarperCollins, $16.99) 978-0-06-072486-3
Can a baby rabbit and a cat used to ruling
the household coexist peacefully? Warm,
expressive, charcoal and pastel illustrations.
(4–6)

Marla Frazee 2008

## Martha in the Middle

written and ill. by Jan Fearnley
(Candlewick, $16.99) 978-0-7636-3800-9
A mouse discovers the advantages of being
the middle sibling. Watercolor and ink illustrations. (4–6)

## Melrose and Croc: An Adventure to Remember

written and ill. by Emma Chichester Clark
(Walker, $16.95) 978-0-8027-9774-2
A plan to surprise a friend for his birthday
results in a glorious escapade. Vibrant,
expressive illustrations. (4–6)

## Mimi

written and ill. by Carol Baicker-McKee
(Bloomsbury, $15.95) 978-1-59990-065-0
Unique soft-sculpture illustrations and simple text show the emotional ups and downs
of a little pig's day. (4–6)

## Minji's Salon

written and ill. by Eun-hee Choung
(Kane/Miller, $15.95) 978-1-933605-67-8
Minji mirrors her mother's visit to a hair
salon by setting up her own beauty shop at
home. Vivid, animated illustrations. (4–6)

## Mommy Do You Love Me?

by Jeanne Willis, ill. by Jan Fearnley
(Candlewick, $15.99) 978-0-7636-3470-4
Mother hen reassures little chick that no
matter what he does, she still loves him.
Energetic watercolor and ink drawings. (3–5)

##  Monkey and Me

written and ill. by Emily Gravett
(S&S, $15.99) 978-1-4169-5457-6
Imitating different animals, a girl and her toy
monkey play until they are tired. Pencil and
watercolor illustrations. (2–6)

##  My Pup

by Margaret O'Hair,
ill. by Tammie Lyon
(Cavendish, $14.99) 978-0-7614-5389-5
With exuberant illustrations and very simple
rhyme, a young girl describes her pet. (3–5)

## Nanuk Flies Home

by Christa Holtei, ill. by Astrid Vohwinkel
(Eerdmans, $16.00) 978-0-8028-5342-4
A mother polar bear and her cub wander
into a northern Canadian town in search of
food. Based on a true story. (4–6)

## No Mush Today

by Sally Derby, ill. by Nicole Tadgell
(Lee & Low, $17.95) 978-1-60060-238-2
Tired of cornmeal porridge for breakfast and
her bawling baby brother, Nonie decides to
live with her grandma. Warm watercolors.
(4–6)

## Not a Stick

written and ill. by Antoinette Portis
(HarperCollins, $14.89) 978-0-06-112326-9
A young pig creates adventures with a stick
in this clever sequel to Not a Box. Imaginative blue-and-black line drawings. (3–6)

## Old Bear

written and ill. by Kevin Henkes
(Greenwillow, $17.99) 978-0-06-155205-2
Old Bear falls asleep for the winter and
dreams of being a cub frolicking in each of
the four seasons. Watercolor and ink illustrations. (2–5)

## ★On the Farm

by David Elliott, ill. by Holly Meade
(Candlewick, $16.99) 978-0-7636-3322-6
Amusing, pithy poems and brilliant wood-
block prints and watercolors convey warm
farm scenes. (3–5)

## One Watermelon Seed

by Celia Barker Lottridge, ill. by Karen Patkau
(Fitzhenry & Whiteside, $17.95)
978-1-55455-034-0
Help children count from one to ten and
then by tens to 100. Brightly colored, simple
illustrations. (4–6)

## Oodles of Animals
written and ill. by Lois Ehlert
(Harcourt, $17.00) 978-0-15-206274-3
Striking collages and clever short poems
introduce some of the identifying character-
istics of many creatures. (3–7)

## Peekaboo Bedtime
written and ill. by Rachel Isadora
(Putnam, $16.99) 978-0-399-24384-4
Strong pastel illustrations show a small
African-American boy and his family as they
play a bedtime game. (2–4)

## The Pigeon Wants a Puppy!
written and ill. by Mo Willems
(Hyperion, $14.99) 978-0-142310960-0
Pigeon believes that a puppy would be a
perfect companion. But would it? Lively
illustrations. (4–6)

## Princess Baby
written and ill. by Karen Katz
(S&W, $14.99) 978-0-375-84119-4
A little girl is angry because her parents call
her lots of different pet names rather than
her preferred "real" name. Bold, bright illustrations. (3–5)

## Puppies and Piggies
by Cynthia Rylant, ill. by Ivan Bates
(Harcourt, $16.00) 978-0-15-202321-8
Rhyming text describes what animals like
and what a baby loves most—his mother.
Watercolor illustrations enhance the loving
quality. (3–5)

## ★The Rain Stomper
by Addie Boswell, ill. by Eric Velasquez
(Cavendish, $16.99) 978-0-7614-5393-2
Jazmin stomps a rhythm, splashes through
puddles and twirls her baton through the
rain that threatens her parade. Dynamic oil
paintings. (4–8)

## Roadwork
by Sally Sutton, ill. by Brian Lovelock
(Candlewick, $15.99) 978-0-7636-3912-9
Experience the hard work and noise pro-
duced by various trucks while building a
road from start to finish. Energetic text and
illustrations. (3–6)

## Ⓑ Rock-a-Bye Farm
by Diane Johnston Hamm,
ill. by Alexi Natchev
(Little Simon, $7.99) 978-1-4169-3621–3
A farmer rocks baby and his farm animals to
sleep before going to bed himself.
Humorous illustrations. (2–4)

## Sally and the Purple Socks
written and ill. by Lisze Bechtold
(Philomel, $15.99) 978-0-399-24734–7
Sally the duck makes the best out of a pair of
socks that keep getting bigger and bigger.
Humorous gouache illustrations. (4–6)

## Sheep Blast Off!
by Nancy Shaw, ill. by Margot Apple
(HMC, $15.00) 978-0-618-13168-6
Sheep encounter a spaceship and accidently
take off. Simple rhyming text and exuberant
pencil illustrations. (4–6)

## Ⓑ Simms Taback's Safari Animals: A Giant Fold-Out Book
written and ill. by Simms Taback
(Chronicle, $12.95) 978-1-934706-19-0
Elephant, zebra, lion, hippo and giraffe—all
appear in vividly colored fold-out flaps. (0-3)

## Smash! Crash!
by Jon Scieszka, ill. by David
Shannon, Loren Long and David Gordon
(S&S, $16.99) 978-1-4169-4133-0
Jack Truck and Dump Truck Dan, best
friends, help the other denizens of a town
populated by vehicles. (2–5)

## Sometimes You Get What You Want
by Meredith Gary, ill. by Lisa Brown
(HarperCollins, $16.99) 978-0-06-114015-0
Familiar scenes capture the occasions when
you get what you want and when you don't.
(2–4)

## ★Ten Little Fingers and Ten Little Toes
by Mem Fox, ill. by Helen Oxenbury
(Harcourt, $16.00) 978-0-15-206057-2
Catchy rhymes and humor embrace all kinds
of babies and what they have in common.
Subtle watercolors exude character. (3–5)

## Too Many Toys

written and ill. by David Shannon
(Blue Sky, $16.99) 978-0-439-49029-0
A mother and child find a nicely handled
solution to an age-old problem. Cheerful,
brightly colored illustrations. (4–6)

## Trout Are Made of Trees

by April Pulley Sayre, ill. by Kate Endle
(Charlesbridge, $15.95) 978-1-58089-137-0
Lyrical text and vibrant collage illustrations
present an informative science lesson on the
food web. (4–6)

## ★Turtle's Penguin Day

written and ill. by Valeri Gorbachev
(Knopf, $16.99) 978-0-375-84374-7
Little turtle becomes a penguin for a day
after his father reads a bedtme story.
Lighthearted watercolor illustrations. (3–7)

## Uh-oh!

written and ill. by Rachel Isadora
(Harcourt, $16.00) 978-0-15-205765-7
Pastel drawings tell the story of many "uh-oh"
moments in the home of an African-American
family with a young baby boy. (1–3)

## The Ultimate Guide to Grandmas & Grandpas

by Sally Lloyd-Jones, ill. by Michael Emberley
(HarperCollins, $14.99) 978-0-06-075687-1
We all need to know how to treat grandparents. Humorous text and colorful illustrations. (3–5)

## ★A Visitor for Bear

by Bonny Becker,
ill. by Kady MacDonald Denton
(Candlewick, $16.99) 978-0-7636-2807-9
Bear believes he enjoys solitude, but a mouse
slyly changes Bear's mind. Muted watercolor,
ink and gouache illustrations. (4–6)

## ★Wave

ill. by Suzy Lee
(Chronicle, $15.99) 978-0-8118-5924-0
A wordless story depicts a little girl's experience at the beach. Charcoal and acrylic illustrations. (3–5)

## Welcome to the Zoo

ill. by Alison Jay
(Dial, $16.99) 978-0-8037-3177-6
Parents and preschoolers explore a colorful
zoo and witness amusing events. Wordless,
with vivid illustrations, including a zoo map
and details to search for. (3–5)

## What Pet to Get?

written and ill. by Emma Dodd
(Arthur A. Levine, $16.99) 978-0-545-03570-5
A small boy considers various unusual candi-
dates, from an elephant to a polar bear.
Colorful watercolors. (3–5)

## What the Grizzly Knows

by David Elliott, ill. by Max Grafe
(Candlewick, $16.99) 978-0-7636-2778-2
A teddy bear comes to life and takes a young
boy on an adventure in the forest. Soft
watercolors and rhyming text. (3–6)

## Who Made the Morning?

by Jan Godfrey, ill. by Honor Ayres
(New Day, $9.99) 978-0-9798247-0-8
Little bird searches for the creator of the
beautiful morning and has an uplifting experience. (3–5)

## Will Sheila Share?

written and ill. by Elivia Savadier
(Roaring Brook, $12.95) 978-1-59643-289-5
A little girl faces the common childhood
struggle. Humorous watercolor and ink illustrations. (4–6)

## ★Wonder Bear

ill. by Tao Nyeu
(Dial, $17.99) 978-0-8037-3328-2
Join two kids on their amazing adventure in
this vibrantly colored silk-screen wordless
book. (4–7)

## You Were Loved Before You Were Born

by Eve Bunting, ill. by Karen Barbour
(Blue Sky, $16.99) 978-0-439-04061-7
Family and friends prepared lovingly for a
child's birth. Folk art illustrations. (2–5)

## Your Own Big Bed

by Rita M. Bergstein,
ill. by Susan Kathleen Hartung
(Viking, $15.99) 978-0-670-06079-5
Learn how animals are just like children as
they grow into having a special place to
sleep. Warm, colorful illustrations. (3–5)

# FIVE TO NINE

## ADVENTURE AND MYSTERY

### Alex Flint: Super Sleuth: The Niña, the Pinta, and the Vanishing Treasure
by Jill Santopolo
(Orchard, $15.99) 978-0-439-90352-3
Fourth-grader Alex and his friends help his policeman father solve a theft. (7–9)

### The Green Ghost
by Marion Dane Bauer,
ill. by Peter Ferguson
(Random, $11.99) 978-0-375-84083-8
A ghost saves Kaye's family on Christmas Eve and leaves clues to solve an unfinished task. (6–9)

### The Last Gold Diggers
written and ill. by Harry Horse
(Peachtree, $12.95) 978-1-56145-435-8
A series of humorous letters describe Grandfather's adventures in Australia with his opinionated dog while searching for his long-lost brother. (7–11)

### Maybelle Goes to Tea
by Katie Speck, ill. by Paul Rátz de Tagyos
(Henry Holt, $16.95) 978-0-8050-8093-3
What happens when a cockroach ventures out for a tasty treat? Humorous black-and-white illustrations. (5–7)

### ★Spuds
by Karen Hesse, ill. by Wendy Watson
(Scholastic, $16.99) 978-0-439-87993-4
Three siblings are in for a big surprise when they gather potatoes from a farmer's field. Colored ink, gouache, and watercolor illustrations. (5–7)

### We're Off to Look for Aliens
written and ill. by Colin McNaughton
(Candlewick, $15.99) 978-0-7636-3636-4
A book within a book describes looking for aliens. (5–7)

Peter Bailey 2008

## ANIMALS

### Big Brown Bat
written and ill. by Rick Chrustowski
(Henry Holt, $16.95) 978-0-8050-7499-4
The natural history of these common bats is described in clear, informative text. Colored pencil and watercolor wash illustrations. (4–7)

### Dolphins on the Sand
written and ill. by Jim Arnosky
(Putnam, $16.99) 978-0-399-24606-7
A dolphin pod stranded on a sandbar is rescued by humans. Glowing, vibrant acrylic illustrations. (5–7)

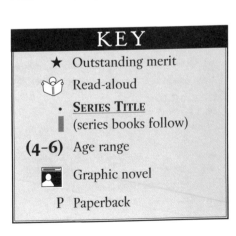

## KEY

★ Outstanding merit

Read-aloud

· **SERIES TITLE**
(series books follow)

(4-6) Age range

Graphic novel

P Paperback

## Hogwood Steps Out: A Good, Good Pig Story

by Howard Mansfield, ill. by Barry Moser (Roaring Brook, $16.95) 978-1-59643-269-7 A very smart pig enjoying the Spring has lots of fun outwitting the humans. Brilliant watercolors. (5–8)

## My Chincoteague Pony

written and ill. by Susan Jeffers (Hyperion, $16.99) 978-1-4231-0023-2 Through hard work and the generosity of strangers, Julie realizes her dream of owning one of the famous ponies. Soft watercolors. (5–8)

## Someone Walks By: The Wonders of Winter Wildlife

written and ill. by Polly Carlson-Voiles (Raven Productions, P$12.95) 978-0-9801045-6-1 Evocative cut-paper illustrations and beguiling text describe animals in winter. (5–9)

## Stella, Unleashed: Notes from the Doghouse

by Linda Ashman, ill. by Paul Meisel (Sterling, $14.95) 978-1-4027-3987-3 An adopted family dog describes her view of the world in rhyme. Playful acrylic illustrations. (6–8)

## Tadpole Rex

written and ill. by Kurt Cyrus (Harcourt, $16.00) 978-0-15-205990-3 Bold, colorful scratchboard illustrations follow a tadpole who grows into a frog during the days of dinosaurs. (6–9)

## BEGINNING READERS

## Andy Shane and the Queen of Egypt

by Jennifer Richard Jacobson, ill. by Abby Carter (Candlewick, $13.99) 978-0-7636-3211-3 Thoughtful Andy and enthusiastic Dolores both want to do a project on Egypt. Will their different styles mesh or clash? (7–9)

## Annie and Snowball and the Pink Surprise

by Cynthia Rylant, ill. by Suçie Stevenson (S&S, $15.99) 978-1-4169-0941-5 A hummingbird comes to Annie's garden. Can she and Henry think of a way to attract more? (6–8)

## Bones and the Math Test Mystery

by David A. Adler, ill. by Barbara Johansen Newman (Viking, $13.99) 978-0-670-06262-1 Jeffrey does not like math, but he is good at solving mysteries. Can he find his missing math test? (5–7)

## Cork and Fuzz: The Collectors

by Dori Chaconas, ill. by Lisa McCue (Viking, $13.99) 978-0-670-06286-7 When best friends Cork, a muskrat, and Fuzz, a possum, go collecting together, trouble comes when Fuzz is "collected" by a mother duck. (5–8)

## Cowgirl Kate and Cocoa: Rain or Shine

by Erica Silverman, ill. by Betsy Lewin (Harcourt, $15.00) 978-0-15-205384-0 In their fourth appearance, Cowgirl Kate and Cocoa remind us that, rain or shine, they are always "just right." (6–8)

## Dogerella

by Maribeth Boelts, ill. by Donald Wu (Random, P$3.99) 978-0-375-83393-9 A fairy dogmother helps Princess Bea and Dogerella find each other in this charming fairy-tale spoof. (6–8)

· ELEPHANT AND PIGGIE

## ★Are You Ready to Play Outside?
## ★I Love My New Toy!
## ★I Will Surprise My Friend!

written and ill. by Mo Willems (Hyperion, $8.99) 978-1-4231-1347-8, 978-1-4231-0961-7, 978-1-4231-0962-4 Two best friends accept the joy of playing with one another. (4–8)

### ★Goose and Duck
by Jean Craighead George,
ill. by Priscilla Lamont
(HarperCollins, $17.89) 978-0-06-117077-5
A boy becomes "mother" to a goose, who
becomes "mother" to a duck, until the birds
grow up. (6–8)

### ★Houndsley and Catina and the Quiet Time
by James Howe, ill. by Marie-Louise Gay
(Candlewick, $14.99) 978-0-7636-3384-4
Houndsley appreciates the peaceful opportunity a snowstorm provides, but Catina frets
that it ruins all her plans. (5–8)

### Jack and the Box
written and ill. by Art Spiegelman
(Toon Books, $12.95) 978-0-09799238-3-8
Jack finds more than he expected in his
"silly toy" box. Clever graphic format. (5–8)

### Max & Mo's Halloween Surprise
by Patricia Lakin, ill. by Brian Floca
(Aladdin, P$3.99) 978-1-4169-2539-2
Two hamsters have a joyous time creating
masks. Appealing cartoon-like line drawings.
(6–8)

### Mercy Watson Thinks Like a Pig
by Kate DiCamillo, ill. by Chris Van Dusen
(Candlewick, $12.99) 978-0-7636-3265-6
Mercy is at it again! She has eaten all the
neighbor's pansies and is in trouble with
Animal Control. Animated gouache illustrations. (6–9)

### ★One Boy
written and ill. by Laura Vaccaro Seeger
(Roaring Brook, $14.95) 978-1-59643-274-1
A counting book full of surprises with
bright, child-like art and clever word play.
(3–6)

### Snow Surprise
by Lisa Campbell Ernst
(Harcourt, $12.95) 978-0-15-206553-9
Joan makes a surprise for her brother, but
some animals have one for her, too. (5–7)

### What's That, Mittens?
by Lola M. Schaefer,
ill. by Susan Kathleen Hartung
(HarperCollins, $16.99) 978-0-06-054662-5
Mittens is bored until he hears a noise.
Bright watercolors with simple repetitive
text. (5–7)

## COMING OF AGE

• AMY HODGEPODGE

### Amy HodgePodge All Mixed Up!
### Amy HodgePodge Happy Birthday to Me
by Kim Wayans and Kevin Kotts,
ill. by Soo Jeong
(Grosset, P$4.99) 978-0-448-44854-1,
978-0-448-44855-8
Formerly homeschooled, Amy, the new girl
in fourth grade, faces her own fears and
successfully confronts teasing while making
good friends. (8–10)

### The Best Story
by Eileen Spinelli, ill. by Anne Wilsdorf
(Dial, $16.99) 978-0-8037-3055-7
When a young girl enters a story writer's
contest, she solicits ideas, but discovers that
the best ones are her own. Humorous watercolor and ink illustrations. (6–8)

### Bloom!: A Little Book About Finding Love
written and ill. by Maria Van Lieshout
(Feiwel, $12.95) 978-0-312-36913-2
Delicate ink and watercolor illustrations with
spare text design show how one little pig
finds love in unexpected places. (3–6)

### Catching the Sun
by Coleen M. Paratore,
ill. by Peter Catalanotto
(Charlesbridge, $16.95) 978-1-57091-720-2
As Dylan shares an early morning adventure
with his mom, he has mixed feelings about
the impending arrival of a new sibling. (5–8)

## ...COMING OF AGE

### The Chicken of the Family
by Mary Amato, ill. by Delphine Durand
(Putnam, $16.99) 978-0-399-24196-3
Her sisters' taunts backfire when Henrietta
is actually convinced she's not a girl, but a
chicken. Funny, stylized paintings. (5–8)

### ★Clementine's Letter
by Sara Pennypacker,
ill. by Marla Frazee
(Hyperion, $14.99) 978-0-7868-3884-4
Clementine helps the substitute teacher learn
the "rules" of her third-grade classroom. (6–8)

### Ellie McDoodle: New Kid in School
written and ill. by Ruth McNally Barshaw
(Bloomsbury, $12.99) 978-1-59990-238-8
To keep track of their move, a family keeps a
journal. Strong, humorous voices. (8–10)

### Her Mother's Face
by Roddy Doyle, ill. by Freya Blackwood
(Arthur A. Levine, $16.99) 978-0-439-81501-7
After her mother dies, Siobhan and her
father mourn for years—until a mysterious
woman offers good advice. (7–10)

### How to Talk to Girls
by Alec Greven
(HarperCollins, $9.99) 978-0-06-170999-9
An experienced nine-year-old boy offers
advice on how to talk to the opposite sex.
(6–10)

### Keena Ford and the Second-Grade Mix-Up
by Melissa Thomson, ill. by Frank Morrison
(Dial, $14.99) 978-0-8037-3263-6
Bubbly Keena can't wait for second grade to
start, but she needs her journal when small
mishaps start to build. (7–9)

### Molly and her Dad
by Jan Ormerod and Carol Thompson
(Roaring Brook, $17.95) 978-1-59643-285-7
When a father who lives far away visits his
daughter, both discover how much they have
in common. Humorous, animated illustrations. (5–8)

### Moxy Maxwell Does Not Love Writing Thank-You Notes
by Peggy Gifford, photos by Valorie Fisher
(S&W, $12.99) 978-0-375–84270-2
Moxy's back and she is not letting twelve
Christmas thank-you notes keep her from
visiting her father in Hollywood. (7–10)

### Puppy Power
by Judy Cox, ill. by Steve Bjorkman
(Holiday House, $15.95) 978-0-8234-2073-5
Third grader Fran works on controlling her
own bossy behavior while teaching her over-
sized Newfoundland puppy, Hercules, to
manage his. (6–8)

### Queen of Halloween
written and ill. by Mary Engelbreit
(HarperCollins, $16.99) 978-0-06-008190-4
While trick-or-treating, Ann and Michael learn
that it takes courage to admit that you are a bit
scared. Humorous illustrations. (4–7)

### Quinito, Day and Night/ Quinito, día y noche
by Ina Cumpiano, ill. by José Ramírez
(Children's Book Press, $16.95)
978-0-89239-226-1
Spend a day with Quinito and learn about
opposites—in English and Spanish. Vibrant,
colorful illustrations. (5–7)

### To the Big Top
by Jill Esbaum, ill. by David Gordon
(FSG, $16.95) 978-0-374-39934-4
When the circus comes to town, two boys
join in the fun and learn about friendship.
Lively illustrations. (7–9)

Peter Bailey 2008

## The Umbrella Queen

by Shirim Yim Bridges, ill. by Taeeun Yoo
(Greenwillow, $16.99) 978-0-06-075040-4
Little Noot, a young Thai girl, dutifully
paints umbrellas, but in her spare time, she
follows her heart. Linoleum print illustrations. (5–8)

## Uncle Monarch and the Day of the Dead

by Judy Goldman, ill. by René King Moreno
(Boyds Mills, $16.95) 978-1-59078-425-9
Lupita must come to terms with the death of
the uncle with whom she celebrated the
annual return of the monarch butterflies.
Soft, colored pencil illustrations. (6–10)

## The Worry Tree

by Marianne Musgrove
(Henry Holt, $15.95) 978-0-8050-8791-8
A discovery behind the wallpaper in her
room helps Juliet solve her problems. (8–10)

## FANTASY

## Hogwash

ill. by Arthur Geisert
(HMC, $16.00) 978-0-618-77332-9
A fantastic pictorial romp illustrates strange
contraptions and machines designed to give
baby pigs a bath. (4–7)

## Magical Kids: The Smallest Girl Ever; The Boy Who Could Fly

written and ill. by Sally Gardner
(Dial, $16.99) 978-0-8037-3159-2
Ten-year-old Ruby and nine-year-old Thomas
develop magical abilities and challenges to
go along with them. (7–9)

## Maybe Later

by Ingrid Lee, ill. by Gabrielle Grimard
(Orca, P$6.95) 978-1-55143-764-4
Johnny's imagination is inspired by an old
green bottle found long ago on the seashore
by his grandfather. (6–9)

## My Friend, the Starfinder

by George Ella Lyon,
ill. by Stephen Gammell
(Atheneum, $16.99) 978-1-4169-2738-9
A neighbor's stories astound a young girl.
But are they true? Fanciful pastel, watercolor, and gouache illustrations. (5–8)

## The Sea Serpent and Me

by Dashka Slater, ill. by Catia Chien
(HMC, $17.00) 978-0-618-723942
A girl cares for an unusual pet and comes to
love the ocean and to accept a loss.
Whimsical watercolors. (5–8)

## Trainstop

written and ill. by Barbara Lehman
(HMC, $16.00) 978-0-618-75640-7
A girl steps off a train into a magic world
and helps the people who ultimately return
the favor. Wordless book with watercolor,
gouache, and ink illustrations. (4–6)

## ★Twenty Heartbeats

by Dennis Haseley, ill. by Ed Young
(Roaring Brook, $16.95) 978-1-59643-238-3
A great painter of horses is commissioned to
capture the beauty of a wealthy man's horse.
Muted collage illustrations. (6–8)

## FOLK AND FAIRY TALES

## The 3 Bears and Goldilocks

by Margaret Willey,
ill. by Heather M. Solomon
(Atheneum, $16.99) 978-1-4169-2494-4
Changing perspectives and detailed illustrations add a new dimension and much humor
to this classic tale. (5–8)

## The Adventures of Sir Lancelot the Great

by Gerald Morris, ill. by Aaron Renier
(HMC, $15.00) 978-0-618-77714-3
This humorous and light-hearted account of
the deeds of King Arthur's bravest knight
brings Camelot alive for young readers. (7–9)

## Anansi and the Box of Stories: A West African Folktale

adapted by Stephen Krensky,
ill. by Jeni Reeves
(Millbrook, $18.95) 978-0-8225-6741-7
Anansi the spider man tricks Nyame the sky
god into sharing with earth's creatures all the
stories in the world. Striking, colorful illustrations. (6–8)

### Anansi's Party Time
by Eric A. Kimmel, ill. by Janet Stevens
(Holiday House, $16.95) 978-0-8234-1922-7
The victim turns the tables on Anansi, the
trickster spider. Humorous mixed-media
illustrations. (5–8)

### The Apple-Pip Princess
written and ill. by Jane Ray
(Candlewick, $16.99) 978-0-7636-3747-7
Who will be the successor to the throne?
The princesses have seven days to prove
their mettle. Folkloric illustrations. (5–7)

### As Luck Would Have It
by Robert D. San Souci,
ill. by Daniel San Souci
(August House, $16.95) 978-0-87483-833-6
Foolish twins wreak havoc on their home
and the family fortune. A rollicking version
of the Grimm tale with lavish watercolors.
(6–8)

### The Fisherman and the Turtle
adapted by Eric A. Kimmel,
ill. by Martha Aviles
(Cavendish, $16.99) 978-0-7614-5387-1
A retelling of the Grimm tale about a fisher-
man and his greedy wife is set in the land of
the Aztecs. Colorful acrylic and watercolor
illustrations. (6–8)

### The Ghost Catcher
by Martha Hamilton and Mitch Weiss,
ill. by Kristen Baloch
(August House, $16.95) 978-0-87483-835-0
In this Bengali tale, a barber, whose wife
presses him to earn money, finds a solution
by tricking a ghost. Simple, colorful illustrations. (7–10)

### Hansel and Gretel
retold by Michael Morpurgo,
ill. by Emma Chichester Clark
(Candlewick, $18.99) 978-0-7636-4012-5
Motives and background are described in
this intelligent, in-depth retelling. Colorful
folk art. (7–10)

Peter Bailey 2008

### Imagine a Dragon
by Laurence Pringle,
ill. by Eujin Kim Neilan
(Boyds Mills, $16.95) 978-1-56397-328-4
Dragon stories from Europe and Asia are
accompanied by swirling detailed acrylic
paintings. (7–10)

### Just in Case: A Trickster Tale and Spanish Alphabet Book
written and ill. by Yuyi Morales
(Roaring Brook, $17.95) 978-1-59643-329-8
Playful English text, peppered with Spanish
and paintings in a vibrant Mexican color
palette, explores an alphabetical gathering of
gifts. (6–8)

### The King Has Goat Ears
by Katarina Jovanovic, ill. by Phillipe Beha
(Tradewind Books, $16.95) 978-1-896580-22-7
A plucky apprentice succeeds in solving the
king's problem when all the other barbers in
the kingdom have failed. Vibrant mixed-
media illustrations. (5–7)

### ★The Magic Pillow
written and ill. by Demi
(McElderry, $19.99) 978-1-4169-2470-8
A poor young boy yearns for wealth and
power until a magician gives him a pillow
that reveals what would happen if his wishes
came true. Traditional Chinese pen-and-
brush paintings.

### The Story Blanket
by Ferida Wolff and Harriet May Savitz,
ill. by Elena Odriozola
(Peachtree, $16.95) 978-1-56145-466-2
A storyteller's blanket becomes the source
for much-needed clothing, but the stories
continue. Colorful watercolors. (5–7)

## Tuko and the Birds: A Tale from the Philippines

by Shirley Climo, ill. by Francisco X. Mora (Henry Holt, $16.95) 978-0-8050-6559-6
When the gecko cries so loudly that the birds cannot sleep, they try to trick him into moving away. (6–9)

## ★Way Up and Over Everything

by Alice McGill, ill. by Judy Daly (HMC, $16.00) 978-0-618-38796-0
Five Africans escape the horrors of slavery by disappearing into air. Graceful watercolors capture the human desire for freedom. (5–8)

## HISTORICAL FICTION

## ★Abe Lincoln Crosses a Creek: A Tall, Thin Tale (Introducing His Forgotten Frontier Friend)

by Deborah Hopkinson, ill. by John Hendrix (S&W, $16.99) 978-0-375–83768-5
Seven-year-old Abe Lincoln falls into a Kentucky creek and is saved by his best friend Austin. Vivid watercolors. (7–10)

## Adèle & Simon in America

written and ill. by Barbara McClintock (FSG, $16.95) 978-0-374-39924-5
Despite his sister's warnings, Simon scatters his belongings all over twentieth-century America. Detailed pen, ink, and watercolor illustrations. (6–9)

## ★The Butter Man

by Elizabeth Alalou and Ali Alalou, ill. by Julie Klear Essakalli (Charlesbridge, $14.95) 978-1-58089-127-1
Hungry for dinner, a girl is transported by her father's tale of his own childhood hunger during a drought. (5–8)

## The Elephant Quilt: Stitch by Stitch to California!

by Susan Lowell, ill. by Stacey Dressen-McQueen (FSG, $16.95) 978-0-374-38223-0
Lily Rose and her brother cross the country in 1859. Along the way, Lily incorporates their adventures into a special memory quilt. (6–8)

## The House of Joyful Living

by Roni Schotter, ill. by Terry Widener (FSG, $16.95) 978-0-374-33429-1
A young girl loves New York apartment life, but becomes jealous when the new baby receives the attention she enjoys. Multicultural illustrations. (5–8)

## Lucy's Cave: A Story of Vicksburg, 1863

written and ill. by Karen B. Winnick (Boyds Mills, $16.95) 978-1-59078-194-4
The true story of eleven-year-old Lucy, who hid with her family and townsfolk in local caves during the Civil War siege. Soulful oil paintings. (7–9)

## ★The Moon Over Star

by Dianna Hutts Aston, ill. by Jerry Pinkney (Dial, $17.99) 978-0-8037-3107-3
At home on the family farm, Mae is inspired by the 1969 moon landing by Apollo astronauts and shares her dreams with a loving grandfather. Magnificent ink and watercolor illustrations. (7–10)

## Night Running: How James Escaped with the Help of His Faithful Dog

by Elisa Carbone, ill. by E. B. Lewis (Knopf, $16.99) 978-0-375-82247-6
When young James escapes from slavery, his hunting dog provides crucial help. Based on a true story. Realistic watercolors. (6–9)

## Ocean Wide, Ocean Deep

by Susan Lendroth, ill. by Raúl Allén (Tricycle, $15.99) 978-1-58246-232-5
Lovely rhymes capture a young girl's feelings about the sea and her father's long, dangerous voyages. (6–8)

## Owney: The Mail-Pouch Pooch

by Mona Kerby, ill. by Lynne Barasch (FSG, $16.95) 978-0-374-35685-9
The amazing travels of the Albany Post Office mascot in the 1890s are inspired by actual events. Colorful watercolors. (6–9)

## ★Priscilla and the Hollyhocks

by Anne Broyles, ill. by Anna Alter
(Charlesbridge, $15.95) 978-1-57091-675-5
A young girl on a southern plantation is sold
and then sold again to a Cherokee family.
After marching on the Trail of Tears, a kind
white man sets her free. (6–9)

## Riding to Washington

by Gwenyth Swain, ill. by David Geister
(Sleeping Bear, $17.95) 978-1-58536-324-7
An historic trip to witness Martin Luther
King's famous speech teaches Janie worth-
while lessons about the world and her per-
sonal values. (6–9)

## ★That Book Woman

by Heather Henson, ill. by David Small
(Atheneum, $16.99) 978-1-4169-0812-8
Based on fact, a story of the impact of the
WPA Librarians on families in remote areas
of Appalachia. Expressive ink and watercol-
or drawings. (5–8)

## Titanicat

by Marty Crisp, ill. by Robert Papp
(Sleeping Bear, $17.95) 978-1-58536-355-1
Based on a first-person account of the fatal
voyage, a cat saves the life of her young Irish
caretaker. Richly colored illustrations. (6–10)

## What to Do About Alice?

by Barbara Kerley,
ill. by Edwin Fotheringham
(Scholastic, $16.99) 978-0-439-92231-9
Alice Roosevelt manages to be a lively and
unconventional spirit despite being President
Theodore Roosevelt's daughter. Author's
notes. Clever digital illustrations. (6–9)

## Yuki and the One Thousand Carriers

by Gloria Whelan, ill. by Yan Nascimbene
(Sleeping Bear, $17.95) 978-1-58536-352-0
Yuki, the young daughter of a Japanese gov-
ernor, comments on her journey to Edo in
haiku. Watercolor paintings evoke ancient
Japan. (7–10)

## Annie and Simon

written and ill. by Catharine O'Neill
(Candlewick, $15.99) 978-0-7636-2688-4
Annie's many antics are patiently supported
by a loving brother. Lighthearted watercolors. (6–8)

## Benny and Penny in Just Pretend

by Geoffrey Hayes
(Toon Books, $12.95) 978-0-9799238-0-7
Benny learns that his kid sister is not such a
bad playmate after all. Lively, colorful graph-
ics. (5–7)

## Big Chickens Fly the Coop

by Leslie Helakoski, ill. by Henry Cole
(Dutton, $15.99) 978-0-525-47915-4
Mayhem ensues when four adventurous
chickens go in search of the farmhouse.
Expressive, colorful illustrations. (4–6)

## Clever Duck

by Dick King-Smith, ill. by Nick Bruel
(Roaring Brook, $15.95) 978-1-59643-327-4
When the conceited pigs start picking on all
the other farm animals, a clever duck and a
dog, seeking revenge, become involved in
amusing adventures. (6–9)

## Cool Zone with the Pain & the Great One

by Judy Blume, ill. by James Stevenson
(Delacorte, $12.99) 978-0-385–73306–9
First grader Jake and his older sister Abigail
have difficulty getting along—but, in the
author's humorous fashion, they resolve their
problems. (5–8)

## ★Crazy Like a Fox: A Simile Story

written and ill. by Loreen Leedy
(Holiday House, $16.95) 978-0-8234-1719-3
The story of Rufus the fox and Babette the
lamb is told entirely in similes. Bright, clever
illustrations. (6–9)

Peter Bailey 2008

## The Day We Danced in Underpants

by Sarah Wilson, ill. by Catherine Stock
(Tricycle, $14.95) 978-1-58246-205-9
A rollicking day is spent with the King of
France when he was a boy. His father and
three aunts join in to get rid of their funny
clothes. Pen and ink, watercolor, and collage
illustrations. (4–7)

## Duck Soup

written and ill. by Jackie Urbanovic
(HarperCollins, $17.89) 978-0-06-121442-4
When Max the duck disappears while con-
cocting his special soup, his friends panic.
Playful, humorous illustrations. (4–7)

## I Know an Old Teacher

by Anne Bowen, ill. by Stephen Gammell
(Carolrhoda, $16.95) 978-0-8225-7984-7
This adaptation of a familiar rhyme is
enhanced by very funny mixed-media illustrations. (6–8)

## Ibby's Magic Weekend

by Heather Dyer, ill. by Peter Bailey
(Chicken House, $16.99) 978-0-545-03209-4
Three cousins have amusing adventures
using a magic set found in their attic. (7–9)

## Little Mouse's Big Book of Fears

written and ill. by Emily Gravett
(S&S, $17.99) 978-1-4169-5930-4
Little mouse fears everything but discovers
that everyone is afraid of some things.
Sophisticated humor is expressed in mock
newsprint and found object collages. (7–10)

## The Pout-Pout Fish

by Deborah Diesen, ill. by Dan Hanna
(FSG, $16.00) 978-0-374-36096-2
Brightly colored ocean creatures offer advice
meant to change the glum expression of
their friend. Playful rhymes and expressive
illustrations. (5–8)

## The Scrambled States of America Talent Show

written and ill. by Laurie Keller
(Henry Holt, $16.95) 978-0-8050-7997-5
The scrambled states are back and they've
put their goofy, wacky talents together in an
unforgettable show. (6–9)

## Snake and Lizard

by Joy Cowley, ill. by Gavin Bishop
(Kane/Miller, $14.95) 978-1-933605-83-8
Two desert creatures overcome their differences and through some humorous misadventures become inseparable friends and
help others. (7–9)

## Stinky

written and ill. by Eleanor Davis
(Toon Book, $12.95) 978-0-9799238-4-5
Stinky the monster plots hilarious ways to
get rid of the kid who enters his swamp.
(6–9)

## Thea's Tree

by Alison Jackson, ill. by Janet Pedersen
(Dutton, $16.99) 978-0-525-47443-2
Thea plants seeds which grow into a tree
that is unidentifiable even to experts.
Humorous illustrations. (6–8)

## Uncle Pirate

by Douglas Rees, ill. by Tony Auth
(McElderry, $15.99) 978-1-4169-4762-2
Wilson, a bullied fourth grader, enjoys helping his long-lost pirate uncle shape up his
chaotic school, pirate style! (7–10)

## SPORTS

## A Girl Named Dan

by Dandi Daley Mackall, ill. by Renée Graef
(Sleeping Bear, $16.95) 978-1-58536-351-3
Despite her talent and passion, Dandi is
excluded from the "boys only" sport of
baseball. Expressive illustrations. (7–9)

## ★A Glove of Their Own

by Debbie Moldovan, Keri Conkling, and Lisa Funari-Willever, ill. by Lauren Lambiase (Franklin Mason Press, $15.95) 978-0-9760469-5-0

This tale, told in verse, celebrates the spontaneity, team play, and the kindness of a man who remembers how it was when baseball was a "pick-up" sport. (7–10)

### • GYM SHORTS

### Basketball Bats
### Goof-Off Goalie
### Swimming with Sharks

by Betty Hicks, ill. by Adam McCauley (Roaring Brook, $15.95) 978-1-59643-244-4, 978-1-59643-243-7, 978-1-59643-245-1

Henry, Goose, Rita, Rocky, and Jaxx love to play a variety of sports and to help each other. (7–9)

## TODAY

### The Best Gift of All

by Jonathan Emmett, ill. by Vanessa Cabban (Candlewick, $15.99) 978-0-7636-3860-3

Mole uses his talent and heart to bring a most special gift to his friend Rabbit. (4–7)

### Eating Enchiladas

by Phyllis Reynolds Naylor, ill. by Marcy Ramsey (Cavendish, $14.99) 978-0-7614-5300-0

Each third grader is supposed to report on a country, but Sarah can't decide until newly-arrived Mercedes gives her an idea. (6–8)

### How to Heal a Broken Wing

written and ill. by Bob Graham (Candlewick, $16.99) 978-0-7636-3903-7

When Will finds a bird with a broken wing, he takes it home and cares for it. Soft pen, watercolor, and chalk illustratons. (5–7)

### Jack's House

by Karen Magnuson Beil, ill. by Mike Wohnoutka (Holiday House, $16.95) 978-0-8234-1913-5

Humorous cumulative text reveals who was really responsible for the house that Jack built. Information about trucks included. (6–8)

### Jim's Dog, Muffins

by Miriam Cohen, ill. by Ronald Himler (Star Bright, $15.95) 978-1-59572-099-3

After his dog is killed, Jim's first-grade classmates try to help him feel better. Sensitive watercolors. (5–7)

### Mermaids on Parade

written and ill. by Melanie Hope Greenberg (Putnam, $16.99) 978-0-399-24708-8

Coney Island's annual festival comes to life through a girl's excitement at being in the parade. Vibrant gouache illustrations. (5–8)

### Metal Man

by Aaron Reynolds, ill. by Paul Hoppe (Charlesbridge, $15.95) 978-1-58089-150-9

A boy watches a neighborhood artist despite his family's reluctance and discovers the beauty of his own imagination. (5–10)

### ★Ms. McCaw Learns to Draw

written and ill. by Kaethe Zemach (Arthur A. Levine, $16.99) 978-0-439-82914-4

Dudley's teacher is really good at helping him pay attention but is really bad at drawing. Lively ink and watercolor illustrations. (5–7)

### My Travelin' Eye

written and ill. by Jenny Sue Kostecki-Shaw (Henry Holt, $16.95) 978-0-8050-8169-5

Because Jenny Sue has a lazy and traveling eye, she sees the world in a special way. Dynamic and humorous illustrations. (6–8)

### One Hen

by Katie Smith Milway, ill. by Eugenie Fernandes (Kids Can, $18.95) 978-1-55453-028-1

The enterprise of a small boy in Ghana flourishes. Acrylic folk art. (7–10)

## A Perfect Season for Dreaming/ Un tiempo perfecto para sonar

by Benjamin Alire Sáenz,
ill. by Esau Andrade Valencia
(Cinco Puntos Press, $17.95)
978-1-933693-01-9
A grandfather shares his fantastic dreams about piñatas. Colorful, folkloric paintings. (7–9)

## Princess Grace

by Mary Hoffman, ill. by
Cornelius Van Wright and Ying-Hwa Hu
(Dial, $16.99) 978-0-8037-3260-5
Grace learns that there are many kinds of princesses as she tries to decide how to compete to be in the school parade. Soft watercolor illustrations. (5–7)

## ★Silent Music: A Story of Baghad

written and ill. by James Rumford
(Roaring Brook, $17.95) 978-1-59643-276-5
Ali endures the Iraqi War by mastering calligraphy. Mixed-media illustrations echo desert colors with Arabic writing flowing through them. (7–10)

## Stanley and the Class Pet

written and ill. by Barney Saltzberg
(Candlewick, $16.99) 978-0-7636-3595-4
Against his better judgment, Stanley lets the class bird out of his cage. Now he must face the consequences. Expressive pencil, ink, and acrylic illustrations. (5–7)

## Two Bobbies: A True Story of Hurricane Katrina, Friendship, and Survival

by Kirby Larson and Mary Nethery,
ill. by Jean Cassels
(Walker, $16.99) 978-0-8027-9754-4
Two abandoned animals help each other through a natural disaster. Based on a true story. (6–9)

## The White Nights of Ramadan

by Maha Addasi, ill. by Ned Gannon
(Boyds Mills, $16.95) 978-1-59078-523-2
Contemporary Kuwaiti children enjoy dressing up, collecting treats, and giving charity to celebrate the "white nights" of the Muslim month of fasting. Vibrant oil paintings. (6–9)

## Yoon and the Jade Bracelet

by Helen Recorvits,
ill. by Gabi Swiatkowska
(FSG, $16.95) 978-0-374-38689-4
Yoon's birthday gifts are not what she hoped for but lead to just what she wants. Expressive oil paintings. (5–8)

# NINE TO TWELVE

## ADVENTURE AND MYSTERY

### The Adventurous Deeds of Deadwood Jones

by Helen Hemphill
(Front Street, $16.95) 978-1-59078-637-6
Thirteen-year-old Prometheus and his cousin
join a cattle drive to find his father, who was
sold away. (10–14)

### All the Lovely Bad Ones: A Ghost Story

by Mary Downing Hahn
(Clarion, $16.00) 978-0-618-85467-7
Travis and Corey plan to revive Fox Hill's
ghosts, only to find that they are the ones
being haunted. (9–12)

### The Case of the Bizarre Bouquets

by Nancy Springer
(Philomel, $14.99) 978-0-399-24518-3
The brilliant sister of Sherlock and Mycroft
solves the Watson kidnapping case using
clever disguises and code-breaking clues.
(9–12)

### The Compound

by S. A. Bodeen
(Feiwel, $16.95) 978-0-312-37015-2
After escaping from an atomic disaster with
his family, Eli manages to solve the mystery
of his entrapment. (10–12)

### ★The Ghosts of Kerfol

by Deborah Noyes
(Candlewick, $16.99) 978-0-7636-3000-3
In 1613, a house is haunted by dead dogs,
jealousy, murder, and vengeance as intertwin-
ing stories move forward in this breathtaking
tale. (10–12)

### Highway Cats

by Janet Taylor Lisle, ill. by David Frankland
(Philomel, $14.99) 978-0-399-25070-5
A band of tough strays reluctantly rescues
three kittens in what becomes a life-changing
experience for the whole town. (8–10)

Harry Horse 1998

### Into the Dark

by Peter Abrahams
(HarperCollins, $17.89) 978-0-06-073709-2
Thirteen-year-old Ingrid's discovery of a
dead man leads to evidence which implicates
her grandfather and challenges her detective
skills. (9–12)

###  ★The London Eye Mystery

by Siobhan Dowd
(David Fickling, $15.99) 978-0-375-84976-3
When Salim disappears into thin air from the
"London Eye," no one wants to take his
cousin Ted's theories seriously. (9–12)

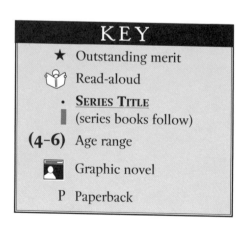

| KEY | |
|---|---|
| ★ | Outstanding merit |
| 🐵 | Read-aloud |
| • | **SERIES TITLE** |
| ▌ | (series books follow) |
| **(4-6)** | Age range |
| 🖼 | Graphic novel |
| P | Paperback |

## Marley Z and the Bloodstained Violin

by Jim Fusilli
(Dutton, $16.99) 978-0-525-47907-9
Accused of stealing a valuable violin, talented Marisol and her friend use their ingenuity to aid the police. (10–13)

## ★ Ottoline and the Yellow Cat

written and ill. by Chris Riddell
(HarperCollins, $10.99) 978-0-06-144879-9
A girl and curiously hairy Mr. Monroe solve the mystery of missing dogs and jewels and catch a thief. Whimsical illustrations. (8–12)

## Paddington Here and Now

by Michael Bond
(HarperCollins, $15.99) 978-0-06-147364-7
In the fiftieth year since his creation, the adopted bear still delights with his hilarious antics. (8–12)

## ★The Seer of Shadows

by Avi
(HarperCollins, $17.89) 978-0-06-000016-5
In New York City in 1872, a fourteen-year-old photography apprentice juggles high society, swindlers, a girlfriend, and a ghost. (9–11)

## Swindle

by Gordon Korman
(Scholastic, $16.99) 978-0-439-90344-8
Will sixth-grader Griffin's plan to retrieve a valuable and extremely well-guarded baseball card succeed? (10–12)

## Tracking Daddy Down

by Marybeth Kelsey
(HarperCollins, $17.89) 978-0-06-128841-8
Eleven-year-old daredevil Billie learns the truth about herself and the adults in her life as she attempts to convince her father to give himself up after robbing a bank. (10–12)

## COMING OF AGE

## 10 Lucky Things That Have Happened to Me Since I Nearly Got Hit by Lightning

by Mary Hershey
(Wendy Lamb, $15.99) 978-0-385-73541-4
After her father's imprisonment, Effie's life has begun to improve, until an old friend of her mother's comes to stay. (9–12)

## ★Along Came Spider

by James Preller
(Scholastic, $15.99) 978-0-545-03299-5
A fifth-grade friendship is put to the test when Trey's special needs come to the fore. (9–12)

## Bird

by Zetta Elliott, ill. by Shadra Strickland
(Lee & Low, $19.95) 978-1-60060-241-2
A young boy deals with great loss through his art, his love of birds, and a strong friendship. (9–11)

## Bird Lake Moon

by Kevin Henkes
(HarperCollins, $15.99) 978-0-06-147076-9
Angry and fearful about his parents' impending divorce, Mitch meets Spencer, who has his own secrets. (9–12)

## ★Brett McCarthy: Work in Progress

by Maria Padian
(Knopf, $15.99) 978-0-375-84675-5
For Brett, junior high brings unexpected and painful changes in relationships, in understandings, and in her sense of self. (9–14)

## The Buddha's Diamonds

by Carolyn Marsden and Thầy Pháp Niệm
(Candlewick, $14.99) 978-0-7636-3380-6
In a small village in Vietnam, Tinh grows emotionally and spiritually in the aftermath of a natural disaster. (10–13)

## The Curse of Addy McMahon

written and ill. by Katie Davis
(Greenwillow, $16.99) 978-0-06-128711-4
Cartoon illustrations advance this story of friendship and major upheavals as twelve-year-old Addy copes with these occurrences. (10–13)

### Diamond Willow
by Helen Frost
(FSG, $16.00) 978-0-374-31776-8
Living in a remote corner of Alaska, twelve-year-old Willow, who loves and is loved by her sled dogs, feels ordinary until an accident changes her world. (9–12)

### Donavan's Double Trouble
by Monalisa DeGross, ill. by Amy Bates
(Amistad, $16.89) 978-0-06-077294-9
The whole family pitches in as Donovan struggles with his feelngs about his favorite uncle, who has returned from war an amputee. (8–10)

### Eleven
by Patricia Reilly Giff
(Wendy Lamb, $15.99) 978-0-385-73069-3
Sam has almost given up on reading and is more interested in pursuing the secret of the attic's locked box. (9–12)

### Flight
by Elizabeth Stow Ellison
(Holiday House, $16.95) 978-0-8234-2128-2
At fourteen, Evan still can't read because he is dyslexic. His sister helps to reveal the problem and develop solutions. (10-12)

### From Alice to Zen and Everyone in Between
by Elizabeth Atkinson
(Carolrhoda, $16.95) 978-0-8225-7271-8
When sixth grader Alice moves to a Boston suburb, she hopes for the best, but making friends is difficult. Her neighbor may not be the best life coach. (9–12)

###  Hate That Cat
by Sharon Creech
(HarperCollins, $16.89) 978-0-06-143093-0
As Jack continues to study poetry, he considers how to share the rich world of sound with his deaf mother. (9–11)

### It's Only Temporary
by Sally Warner
(Viking, $15.99) 978-0-670-06111-2
When her older brother almost dies in an automobile accident, twelve-year-old Skye discovers the value of relationships. (9–12)

### Julia Gillian (and the Art of Knowing)
by Alison McGhee, ill. by Drazen Kozjan
(Scholastic, $15.99) 978-0-545-03348-0
Nine-year-old Julia Gillian of Minneapolis conquers her fears through her "art of knowing," along with her dog Bigfoot's help. (8–10)

### The Last Invisible Boy
by Evan Kuhlman, ill. by J.P. Coovert
(Atheneum, $16.99) 978-1-4169-5797-3
Finn Garrett feels as if he is fading away after the unexpected death of his father. (10–13)

### ★The Leanin' Dog
by K. A. Nuzum
(HarperCollins, $16.89) 978-0-06-113935-2
After the tragic death of her mother, lonely Dessa Dean finds a four-legged friend who is just as needy as she is. (9–12)

### Lizard Love
by Wendy Townsend
(Front Street, $17.95) 978-1-932425-34-5
The discovery of a pet store eases thirteen-year-old Grace's transition from the Midwest to New York City and from childhood to adolescence. (10–13)

### ★Love Me Tender
by Audrey Couloumbis
(Random, $16.99) 978-0-375-83839-2
Embarrassed by her father who imitates Elvis and alienated from her pregnant acid-tongued mother, Elvira, thirteen, eventually learns she is part of a loving family. (10-12)

### Lucky
by Rachel Vail
(HarperCollins, $16.99) 978-0-06-089043-8
Over-the-top plans for an eighth-grade graduation celebration are upset—exposing issues of friendship, sisterhood, first love, and affluence. (11–14)

### ★Manolito Four-Eyes
by Elvira Lindo, ill. by Emilio Urberuaga
(Cavendish, $15.99) 978-0-7614-5303-1
The irrepressible Manolito narrates his humorous adventures with his beloved grandfather in his small Madrid neighborhood. (8–11)

## Memories of Babi
by Aranka Siegal
(FSG, $16.00) 978-0-374-39978-6
A young girl visits her Ukrainian grandmother, whose life and values have a lasting influence on her. (9–13)

## Minn and Jake's Almost Terrible Summer
by Janet S. Wong, ill. by Geneviève Côté
(FSG, $15.00) 978-0-374-34977-6
When Jake returns to the city for the summer, his unlikely friendship with Minn is tested. Light-hearted black-and-white illustrations. (8–11)

## My So-Called Family
by Courtney Sheinmel
(S&S, $15.99) 978-1-4169-5785-0
Thirteen-year-old Leah, conceived by artificial insemination, questions the definitions of what constitutes a family. (9–12)

## The Nine Lives of Travis Keating
by Jill MacLean
(Fitzhenry & Whiteside, P$11.95)
978-1-55455-104-0
After the death of his mother, twelve-year-old Travis must contend with a move, a bully, and a new school, but a colony of feral cats helps him. (9–12)

## The Penderwicks on Gardam Street
by Jeanne Birdsall
(Knopf, $15.99) 978-0-375-84090-6
Four sisters band together to keep their widowed father from dating. (9–11)

## Penina Levine Is a Potato Pancake
by Rebecca O'Connell,
ill. by Majella Lue Sue
(Roaring Brook, $16.95) 978-1-59643-213-0
Many problems surface for Penina at Hanukkah: an annoying little sister, along with a favorite teacher and her best friend both leaving. (8–12)

## Sarah Simpson's Rules for Living
by Rebecca Rupp
(Candlewick, $13.99) 978-0-7636-3220-5
Through her humorous and thoughtful lists and a class play, plucky Sara learns to accept her parents' divorce. (8–12)

## A Thousand Never Evers
by Shana Burg
(Delacorte, $15.99) 978-0-385-73470-7
In 1963, twelve-year-old Addie shares the trials and tribulations that personalize the civil rights struggle in her small Mississippi town. (9–12)

## The Totally Made-Up Civil War Diary of Amanda MacLeish
by Claudia Mills
(FSG, $16.00) 978-0-374-37696-3
At school, ten-year-old Amanda studies the period when the nation was divided, while at home her own family is breaking apart. (9–11)

## The Truth about My Bat Mitzvah
by Nora Raleigh Baskin
(S&S, $15.99) 978-1-4169-3558-2
Caroline struggles with her Jewish identity after the death of her beloved grandmother. (9–13)

## Ways to Live Forever
by Sally Nicholls
(Arthur A. Levine, $16.99)
978-0-545-06948-9
Eleven-year-old Sam McQueen, suffering from leukemia, chronicles his life, family, and dreams. (9–12)

## Word Nerd
by Susin Nielsen
(Tundra, $18.95) 978-0-88776-875-0
Twelve-year-old Ambrose is allergic, awkward, and over-protected. When he needs something to take pride in, a Scrabble club proves just the thing. (10–13)

## FANTASY

 **Airman**
by Eoin Colfer
(Hyperion, $17.99) 978-142310750-7
In this adventurous 1890s alternative history, teenager Conor has lived a charmed life until he is wrongly accused and unjustly imprisoned. (10–12)

**Aurelie: A Faerie Tale**
by Heather Tomlinson
(Henry Holt, $16.95) 978-0-8050-8276-0
Princess Aurelie and her good friends Netta and Gavin are key players in the battle between two warring kingdoms. (9–11)

**The Cabinet of Wonders**
by Marie Rutkoski
(FSG, $16.95) 978-0-374-31026-4
When her father's eyes are stolen by the Prince of Prague, Petra tries to retrieve them in the face of great danger. (10–13)

**Chalice**
by Robin McKinley
(Putnam, $18.99) 978-0-399-24676-0
Mirasol, newly appointed as Chalice to a frightening new Master, listens to the land and her bees in this suspenseful, romantic adventure. (9–12)

**Dolphin Song**
by Lauren St. John
(Dial, $16.99) 978-0-8037-3214-8
After being tossed off a boat in a storm, an orphaned South African eleven-year-old is rescued by dolphins. (10–12)

**★Ghost Letters**
by Stephen Alter
(Bloomsbury, $16.95) 978-1-58234-739-4
Mysterious, undelivered old letters confound time travelers with supernatural overtones that link late nineteenth-century India with present-day Massachusetts. (9–12)

**The Girl Who Could Fly**
by Victoria Forester
(Feiwel, $16.95) 978-0-312-37462-4
When nine-year-old Piper discovers she can fly, the freedom-seeking child is set against a fearful, unimaginative world. (8–11)

**Gods of Manhattan**
by Scott Mebus
(Dutton, $17.99) 978-0-525-47955-0
A hidden world of Gods, ancient Indians, and talking cockroaches lures twelve-year-old Rory into a dangerous mission. (9–14)

**The Graveyard Book**
by Neil Gaiman, ill. by Dave McKean
(HarperCollins, $17.99) 978-0-06-053092-1
Nobody Owens, raised by ghosts in an abandoned graveyard, needs to discover if he is capable of being Somebody. (9–13)

 **Kenny and the Dragon**
written and ill. by Tony DiTerlizzi
(S&S, $15.99) 978-1-4169-3977-1
When the king enlists George to fight the dragon menacing Roundbrook, Kenny must use his wits to save the day. (8–10)

**Masterpiece**
by Elise Broach, ill. by Kelly Murphy
(Henry Holt, $16.95) 978-0-8050-8270-8
Lonely eleven-year-old James becomes the center of attention when Marvin the beetle creates art in the style of Dürer. (9–13)

**Medusa Jones**
written and ill. by Ross Collins
(Arthur A. Levine, $16.99) 978-0-439-90100-0
Can the young snake-haired Medusa of Athens keep her promise not to turn her enemies into stone? Black-and-white pencil illustrations (8–12)

**Monsterology: The Complete Book of Monstrous Beasts**
edited by Dugald A. Steer
(Candlewick, $19.99) 978-0-7636-3940-2
Scientific methodology is applied to the discovery of monsters in this imaginative journey. Detailed illustrations and text. (9–12)

**Moribito: Guardian of the Spirit**
by Nahoko Uehashi, ill. by Yuko Shimizu, trans. by Cathy Hirano
(Arthur A. Levine, $17.99) 978-0-545-00542-5
The bodyguard, Balsa, must battle monsters and royal enemies to save the life of a prince and a land from drought. (10–13)

## Spellbound

by Anna Dale
(Bloomsbury, $16.99) 978-1-59990-006-3
Caught by magical creatures, Athene and her little brother are trapped in an underground civilization. (8–11)

## ★The Swan Kingdom

by Zoë Marriott
(Candlewick, $16.99) 978-0-7636-3481-0
With some elements of Andersen's "The Wild Swans," this story of a young woman slowly learning about her inherited powers is deeply magical. (10–14)

## Up and Down the Scratchy Mountains

by Laurel Snyder
(Random, $16.99) 978-0-375-84719-6
An adventure for Lucy, a milkmaid, and her friend Wynston, a prince, is filled with wonder, songs, and mystery. (8–10)

## FOLK AND FAIRY TALES

## The Book of Wizards

selected and illustrated by Michael Hague
(HarperCollins, $19.99) 978-0-688-14005-2
Merlin, Prospero, and Baba Yaga join lesser-known magicians from around the world. Pen-and-ink and color illustrations. (8–12)

## Dance, Nana, Dance/ Baila, Nana, Baila: Cuban Folktales in English and Spanish

retold by Joe Hayes,
ill. by Mauricio Trenard Sayago
(Cinco Punto, $20.95) 978-1-933693-17-0
Cuban culture shines through this lively collection of folktales about wisdom, wealth, tricksters, and devils. (9–12)

##  The McElderry Book of Greek Myths

retold by Eric A. Kimmel,
ill. by Pep Montserrat
(McElderry, $21.99) 978-1-4169-1534-8
Pandora's box of hope, Arachne's special weave, and the wax wings of Icarus come to life in this elegant collection. Dramatic illustrations. (8–10)

## More Bones: Scary Stories from Around the World

selected and retold by Arielle North Olson and Howard Schwartz, ill. by E. M. Gist
(Viking, $15.99) 978-0-670-06339-0
Twenty-two spooky tales from China to Egypt, from Spain to Hawaii. (8–12)

## • MYTHS OF THE WORLD

## The Ancient Egyptians
## The Ancient Greeks
## The Native Americans
## The Norsemen

written by Virginia Schomp,
maps by Mike Regan
(Cavendish, $22.95) 978-0-7614-2549-6,
978-0-7614-2547-2, 978-0-7614-2548-9,
978-0-7614-2550-2
A retelling of several myths with background information describing the history, geography, and belief systems of each. (10–14)

## Trick of the Tale: A Collection of Trickster Tales

by John & Caitlin Matthews,
ill. by Tomislav Tomic
(Candlewick, $18.99) 978-0-7636-3646-3
Tricksters from around the world outwit their fellow creatures using all the clever techniques they can summon. Expressive black-and-white engravings. (9–12)

Marla Frazee 2008

# HISTORICAL FICTION

## ★Always with You
by Ruth Vander Zee, ill. by Ronald Himler
(Eerdmans, $17.00) 978-0-8028-5295-3
A moving account of a child's survival against terrible odds during the Vietnam War is accompanied by poignant watercolor and pencil illustrations. (8–12)

## The Bear Makers
by Andrea Cheng
(Front Street, $16.95) 978-1-59078-518-8
In post World War II Hungary, Kata and her family struggle to survive, hoping for a better future. (9–12)

## A Boy Named Beckoning: The True Story of Dr. Carlos Montezuma, Native American Hero
adapted and ill. by Gina Capaldi
(Carolrhoda, $16.95) 978-0-8225-7644-0
Sold into slavery, Dr. Carlos Montezuma overcomes incredible obstacles to become a doctor and an advocate for Native American rights. (9–11)

## Boycott Blues: How Rosa Parks Inspired a Nation
by Andrea Pinkney, ill. by Brian Pinkney
(Greenwillow, $17.89) 978-0-082119-7
A poetic and poignant text recalls the 1955 event which inspired civil rights in the United States. Swirling colored ink illustrations. (9–12)

James Stevenson 2008

## ★Brooklyn Bridge

by Karen Hesse
(Feiwel, $17.95) 978-0-312-37886-8
In Brooklyn in 1903, Joseph's comfortable family life contrasts with those who find refuge under the Brooklyn Bridge. (10–14)

## The Dragonfly Pool
by Eva Ibbotson,
ill. by Kevin Hawkes
(Dutton, $17.99) 978-0-525-42064-4
During World War II, eleven-year-old Tally rescues a prince from the Nazis with the help of her friends. (9–12)

## ★The Dragon's Child: A Story of Angel Island
by Laurence Yep, with Dr. Kathleen S. Yep
(HarperCollins, $16.89) 978-0-06-027693-5
Life in rural China and the subsequent move to America is depicted in this tale based on the life of the author's family. (10–12)

## The Golden Bull
by Marjorie Cowley
(Charlesbridge, $15.95) 978-1-58089-181-3
In ancient Mesopotamia, fourteen-year-old Joman and his sister Zefa survive by learning new skills and reaffirming their love for each other. (8–10)

## The Hope Chest
by Karen Schwabach
(Random, $16.99) 978-0-375-84095-1
In 1917, eleven-year-old Violet learns about women's suffrage from her rebellious sister, who refuses to follow the traditional woman's role. (9–12)

## Juliet's Moon
by Ann Rinaldi
(Harcourt, $17.00) 978-0-15-206170-8
Juliet, captured by Yankees because her brother is a Confederate War bushwhacker, must find her way between the danger posed by both sides. (10–13)

## The Letter Writer
by Ann Rinaldi
(Harcourt, $17.00) 978-0-15-206402-0
Harriet unwittingly supplies Nat Turner, the seemingly mild-mannered slave preacher, with information vital to the bloody rebellion. (9–12)

## Little Audrey

by Ruth White
(FSG, $16.00) 978-0-374-34580-8
In 1948, eleven-year-old Audrey deals with the hardships in a Virginia coal mining camp and discovers her own voice. (9–12)

## The Porcupine Year

by Louise Erdrich
(HarperCollins, $16.89) 978-0-06-029788-6
Omakayas' family has been uprooted by the U.S. Government and must move West. Surviving a tough year, Omakayas becomes a strong and compassionate woman. (9–14)

## Private Joel and the Sewell Mountain Seder

by Bryna J. Fireside, ill. by Shawn Costello
(Kar-Ben, P$6.95) 978-0-8225-9050-7
A Jewish Union soldier and three freed slaves plan a Seder meal to celebrate Passover, the Festival of Freedom. Based on a true story. (9–11)

## Quest: A World of Discovery. . . One Fateful Voyage

by Kathleen Benner Duble
(McElderry, $16.99) 978-1-4169-3386-1
Deprivation at home and at sea mark Henry Hudson's fateful voyage aboard the Discovery early in the seventeenth century. (10–12)

## The Redheaded Princess

by Ann Rinaldi
(HarperCollins, $16.89) 978-0-06-073375-9
The future Queen Elizabeth tells of her life from the age of nine until she ascends the throne at twenty-five. (9–13)

## Secrets of the Cirque Medrano

by Elaine Scott
(Charlesbridge, $15.95) 978-1-57091-712-7
Brigitte, an orphan, finds a home in a Montmartre café frequented by Picasso, his circle, and performers in a nearby circus. (9–12)

## Sisters of the Sword

by Maya Snow
(HarperCollins, $16.99) 978-0-06-124387-5
When their uncle kills their father, two Japanese sisters leave their home. Pretending to be boys, they study at a school for samurai. (10–12)

## Who's Jim Hines?

by Jean Alice Elster
(Wayne State University Press, P$12.95) 978-0-8143-3402-7
Proud of his father, owner of a lumber yard, a black twelve-year-old confronts racial injustice in Detroit during the Depression. (9–12)

# HUMOR

## Antsy Does Time

by Neal Shusterman
(Dutton, $16.99) 978-0-525-47825-6
A friend with a weird disease and a beautiful older sister inspires an eighth-grade Brooklyn boy to find a creative way to help. (10–13)

## Chess! I Love It I Love It I Love It!

by Jamie Gilson, ill. by Amy Wummer
(Clarion, $15.00) 978-0-618-97790-1
Follow the entertaining fortunes of an elementary school chess club. Expressive black-and-white illustrations. (8–10)

## I Put a Spell on You: From the Files of Chrissie Woodward, Spelling Bee Detective

by Adam Selzer
(Delacorte, $15.99) 978-0-385-73504-9
The annual spelling bee creates a competitive environment for an unusual cohort of sixth graders. (10–12)

## The Joy of Spooking: Fiendish Deeds

by P. J. Bracegirdle
(McElderry, $15.99) 978-1-4169-3416-5
Greedy politicians want to turn Spooking Bog into a water park, but intrepid Joy Wells has other ideas. (9–11)

## Oggie Cooder

by Sarah Weeks
(Scholastic, $16.99) 978-0-439-92791-8
Quirky fourth grader Oggie Cooder has one major talent that could get him on television—and in a whole lot of trouble. (8–10)

## ...HUMOR

### The Pirates of Turtle Rock
by Richard W. Jennings
(HMC, $16.00) 978-0-618-98793-1
A modern-day teen pirate meets a bored girl, and together they find love and treasure in a madcap adventure. (11–13)

### Twice Upon a Marigold: Part Comedy, Part Tragedy, Part Two
by Jean Ferris
(Harcourt, $17.00) 978-0-15-206382-5
In this zany sequel, the unpopular queen returns to the castle and threatens the newly-weds and the entire kingdom. Will they be able to thwart her evil plans? (9–12)

### ★The Willoughbys
written and ill. by Lois Lowry
(HMC, $16.00) 978-0-618-97974-5
An old-fashioned novel with much humor and many bizarre happenings is presented as a spoof. Superb glossary and bibliography. (8–12)

## SCIENCE FICTION

###  The Attack of the Frozen Woodchucks
by Dan Elish, ill. by Greg Call
(HarperCollins, $17.89) 978-0-06-113871-3
Ten-year-old Jimmy and his sidekicks William and Janice use their scientific expertise to battle extraterrestrial wood-chucks. (9–12)

### The Diamond of Darkhold
by Jeanne DuPrau
(Random, $16.99) 978-0-375-85571-9
Lina and Doon discover a source of electricity for the people of Sparks. Fourth and last book in the City of Ember series. (9–12)

### Found
by Margaret Peterson Haddix
(S&S, $15.99) 978-1-4169-5417-0
Two adopted friends find out about their origins and uncover a time travel mystery. (9–12)

### Lost Time
by Susan Maupin Schmid
(Philomel, $16.99) 978-0-399-24460-5
A twelve-year-old girl seeks her lost parents while battling aliens and a planet dictator. (9–12)

## SPORTS

### Baseball Crazy: Ten Stories That Cover All the Bases
edited by Nancy E. Mercado
(Dial, $16.99) 978-0-8037-3162-2
Whether you're on the mound, at the plate, warming the benches, or cheering in the stands, it's all about the national pastime. (9–12)

### Beanball
by Gene Fehler
(Clarion, $16.00) 978-0-618-84348-0
A near-fatal baseball injury causes a range of reactions, including fifteen-year-old Luke's need to examine his own feelings and relationships. (10–14)

### ★The Big Field
by Mike Lupica
(Philomel, $17.99) 978-0-399-24625-8
A talented fourteen-year-old baseball player feels betrayed when he sees his father coach the new teammate who "demoted" him from his beloved shortstop position. (10–14)

### Boost
by Kathy Mackel
(Dial, $16.99) 978-0-8037-3240-7
Thirteen-year-old Savvy must cope with both making the basketball team in a new state and the jealousy of her beautiful younger sister. (10–12)

###  ★Keeping Score
by Linda Sue Park
(Clarion, $16.00) 978-0-618-92799-9
In 1950s Brooklyn, eleven-year-old Maggie learns that a serious world exists beyond that of her beloved Dodgers. (9–12)

## Long Shot
## Safe at Home
by Mike Lupica
(Philomel, $9.99) 978-0-399-24717-0,
978-0-399-24716-3
Middle school basketball and baseball are described in depth and with a ring of truth. (8–11)

## ★No Cream Puffs
by Karen Day
(Wendy Lamb, $15.99) 978-0-375-83775-3
The question in Madison's hometown in 1980 is whether a twelve-year-old girl can play on a boy's baseball team. (9–12)

## Six Innings
by James Preller
(Feiwel, $16.95) 978-0-312-36763-3
This play-by-play of a Little League championship game includes vignettes of its players and their families—and of Sam, who is benched because he has cancer. (9–12)

## TODAY

## Acting Out:
## Six One-Act Plays!
## Six Newbery Stars!
by Avi, Susan Cooper, Sharon Creech, Patricia MacLachlan, Katherine Paterson
(Atheneum, $16.99) 978-1-4169-3848-4
Whether they're about Edgar Allan Poe at twelve or dancing in detention, the plays in this collection make for a great read and give readers an incentive to perform. (9–12)

## Dear Toni
by Cyndi Sand-Eveland
(Tundra, $14.95) 978-0-88776-876-7
It's hard being the "new girl" and trying to make friends in another school, but an imaginary girl in a journal assignment helps Gene cope. (9–12)

## Libertad
by Alma Fullerton
(Fitzhenry & Whiteside, P$11.95)
978-1-55455-106-4
After his mother's death, a Guatemalan boy and his little brother struggle to get to the U.S. and find their father. Vividly told in verse. (10–13)

## The Patron Saint of Butterflies
by Cecilia Galante
(Bloomsbury, $16.99) 978-1-59990-249-4
Two fourteen-year-old girls, in a religious commune since birth, must reconsider their lives and beliefs when allegations of abuse arise. (11–13)

## The Tallest Tree
by Sandra Belton
(Amistad, $17.89) 978-0-06-052750-1
A hero gives little Catfish hope for the future and revives the spirit of a small town. (8–11)

## Waiting for Normal
by Leslie Connor
(HarperCollins, $17.89) 978-0-06-089089-6
A spirited, self-reliant twelve-year-old copes with living with her irresponsible mother after being separated from her loving stepfather and half-sisters. (10–12)

## Where the Steps Were
by Andrea Cheng
(Wordsong, $16.95) 978-1-932425-88-8
Facing the closure of their school, five third graders in Miss D's class share the details of their lives. In verse. (8–10)

## Write Before Your Eyes
by Lisa Williams Kline
(Delacorte, $15.99) 978-0-385-73568-1
Diary entries coming true? Whether by "magic" or coincidence, Gracie's jottings cause her friends serious problems. (10–12)

# TWELVE TO FOURTEEN

James Stevenson 2008

## ADVENTURE AND MYSTERY

### Catcall
by Linda Newbery
(David Fickling, $15.99) 978-0-385-75164-3
In this British psychological thriller, cat-loving Josh struggles to understand why a lion has taken over his younger brother's life. (11–14)

### The Diamond of Drury Lane
by Julia Golding
(Roaring Brook, $16.95) 978-1-59643-351-9
Cat Royal becomes involved in eighteenth-century political intrigue and is pursued by a street gang before noble friends come to the rescue. (11–14)

### The Door of No Return
by Sarah Mussi
(McElderry, $17.99) 978-1-4169-1550-8
Ruthlessly pursued, Zac must solve the mystery of his grandfather's murder and the truth of his own ancestry among the Ghanian Kings. (12–15)

### The Entertainer and the Dybbuk
by Sid Fleischman
(Greenwillow, $17.89) 978-0-06-134446-6
A ventriloquist develops a transforming relationship with the spirit of a twelve-year-old Jewish victim of the Nazis. (11–14)

### The Mystery of the Third Lucretia
by Susan Runholt
(Viking, $16.99) 978-0-670-06252-2
Two teenage girls discover a major art forgery and murder scheme. (12–15)

### Nick of Time: An Adventure Through Time
by Ted Bell
(St. Martin's, $17.95) 978-0-312-38068-2
Nick McIver's bravery and knowledge of the sea help him cope with both nineteenth-century pirates and Nazi U-boats. (11–14)

### ★Savvy
by Ingrid Law
(Dial, $16.99) 978-0-8037-3306-0
Thirteen-year-old Mibs uses her new powers to help her critically injured father and acquires friends and understanding. (11–13)

## COMING OF AGE

### 42 Miles
by Tracie Vaughn Zimmer,
ill. by Elaine Clayton
(Clarion, $16.00) 978-0-618-61867-5
Can twelve-year-old Jo Ellen turn the two halves of her joint-custody, city/country life into one whole? Told in free verse with mixed-media illustrations. (11–13)

## KEY

★ Outstanding merit

📖 Read-aloud

**(4–6)** Age range

Ⓜ Mature

👤 Graphic novel

P Paperback

## ★After Tupac & D Foster
by Jacqueline Woodson
(Putnam, $15.99) 978-0-399-24654-8
Tupac Shakur's music and tragic life form a backdrop to this warm story of friendship among three girls in Queens. (12–14)

## Alive and Well in Prague, New York
by Daphne Grab
(HarperCollins, $16.99) 978-0-06-125670-7
Teenage Matisse is embarrassed by her father's advancing Parkinson's disease. (12–14)

## All Shook Up
by Shelley Pearsall
(Knopf, $15.99) 978-0-375-83698-5
His dad's embarrassing new job makes the challenge of adjusting to a new school particularly hard for thirteen-year-old Josh. (11–14)

## Beneath My Mother's Feet
by Amjed Qamar
(Atheneum, $16.99) 978-1-4169-4728-8
When the family falls on harder times, Nazia leaves school and goes to work with her mother as a maid. (12–16)

## ★Every Soul a Star
by Wendy Mass
(Little, $15.99) 978-0-316-00256-1
Three friendships begin while a crowd gathers to catch a glimpse of the total eclipse of the sun. (11–13)

## Ⓜ Fact of Life #31
by Denise Vega
(Knopf, $16.99) 978-0-375-84819-3
Sixteen-year-old Kat struggles because her mother, a midwife, seems to care more deeply for her clients than for her daughter. (13–14)

## First Time
by Meg Tilly
(Orca, P$9.95) 978-1-55143-944-0
Teenager Lynn copes with the unwanted overtures of her mother's new boyfriend. How can she ruin her mother's happiness by telling her? (12–14)

## ★The Ghost's Child
by Sonya Hartnett
(Candlewick, $16.99) 978-0-7636-3964-8
An old woman shares her fanciful story with a young visitor in this beautiful, fable-like quest for the meaning of life. (13–15)

## Good Enough
by Paula Yoo
(HarperCollins, $17.89) 978-0-06-079089-9
As her educated family members endure the humiliation of being outsiders, a Korean-American teenager strives to fulfill their demand for perfection. (12–14)

## ★He Forgot to Say Goodbye: The Things Our Fathers Left Unsaid
by Benjamin Alire Sáenz
(S&S, $16.99) 978-1-4169-4963-3
Two unlikely teens find an unusual bond; they are both fatherless. (12–16)

## ★House of Dance
by Beth Kephart
(HarperCollins, $16.99) 978-0-06-142928-6
Fifteen-year-old Rosie gives a life-affirming gift to her dying grandfather. (12–15)

## How Not to Be Popular
by Jennifer Ziegler
(Delacorte, $15.99) 978-0-385-73465-3
Moving all the time means losing friends over and over. This time Maggie decides just not to make any. (12–14)

## Itch
by Michelle D. Kwasney
(Henry Holt, $16.95) 978-0-8050-8083-4
While seeking help after the loss of her grandfather, Itch finds someone who is suffering more than she is. (11–14)

## Jerk, California
by Jonathan Friesen
(Penguin, P$9.99) 978-0-14-241203-9
On the road, Jack gains a sense of the father he never knew and the confidence to combat his Tourette's syndrome. (12–16)

### Joseph
by Shelia P. Moses
(McElderry, $16.99) 978-1-4169-1752-6
Fifteen-year-old Joseph tries to protect and
care for his alcoholic and drug-addicted
mother while finding his own identity.
(12–16)

### The Landing
by John Ibbitson
(Kids Can, $17.95) 978-1-55453-234-6
Ben is trapped in a poverty-stricken island
existence until a wealthy summer visitor rec-
ognizes and encourages his musical talent.
(12–15)

### Love & Lies: Marisol's Story
by Ellen Wittlinger
(S&S, $16.99) 978-1-4169-1623-9
Marisol defers college for a year to write a
novel and experiences the ups and downs of
new love—lesbian and straight. (12–14)

### Ⓜ Madapple
by Christina Meldrum
(Knopf, $16.99) 978-0-375-85176-6
When home-schooled, teenage Aslaug's
mother dies, she finds relatives, family
secrets, and more. (12–14)

### My Most Excellent Year: A Novel of Love, Mary Poppins & Fenway Park
by Steve Kluger
(Dial, $16.99) 978-0-8037-3227-8
Three creative ninth graders prove that while
some situations are very challenging, nothing
is impossible. (12–14)

### Outside Beauty
by Cynthia Kadohata
(Atheneum, $16.99) 978-0-689-86575-6
Four sisters, with four different fathers and a
charismatic but unpredictable mother, cope
with an accident that threatens their unique
family. (12–14)

### Owning It: Stories About Teens with Disabilities
edited by Donald R. Gallo
(Candlewick, $17.99) 978-0-7636-3255-7
Medical challenges that teens may face are
described honestly and realistically by noted
authors of teen fiction. (12–14)

### Ⓜ Piggy
by Mireille Geus, trans. by Nancy Forest-Flier
(Front Street, $14.95) 978-1-59078-636-9
When autistic twelve-year-old Lizzy makes
friends with an emotionally disturbed girl,
devastating events unfold that challenge her
inner resources. (11–14)

### Puppy Love
by Nancy Krulik
(S&S, P$6.99) 978-1-4169-6152-9
High school senior Alana spends time helping both dogs and people, but she still reacts
to well-developed abs. (11–13)

### ★Ⓜ The Running Man
by Michael Gerard Bauer
(Greenwillow, $16.99) 978-0-06-145508-7
14-year-old Joseph visits his reclusive neighbor to draw his portrait, and helps him come
out of his cocoon just as his silkworm
emerges. (12–14)

### Shift
by Jennifer Bradbury
(Atheneum, $16.99) 978-1-4169-4732-5
When Chris and Win bicycle from West
Virginia to the Pacific, each boy learns more
about himself and the loyalty of true friends.
(11–15)

### Slipping
by Cathleen Davitt Bell
(Bloomsbury, $16.95) 978-1-59990-258-6
Michael's odd and frightening connection to
his dead grandfather leads him to a greater
understanding of his father, his friends, and
himself. (11–13)

### Ⓜ Where People Like Us Live
by Patricia Cumbie
(HarperCollins, $16.99) 978-0-06-137597-2
Should fourteen-year-old Libby reveal her
friend's painful secret—and risk destroying
their friendship? (13–14)

### ⓂWould You
by Marthe Jocelyn
(Wendy Lamb, $15.99) 978-0-375-83703-6
Natalie must grapple with life and death
issues when her sister's accident leaves her
on life support. (13–15)

## FANTASY

### Bewitching Season
by Marissa Doyle
(Henry Holt, $16.95) 978-0-8050-8251-7
In 1837, seventeen-year-old twins, ready to
enter London society, use their gifts of magic
to prevent quackery against Princess
Victoria. (11–14)

### ★Black Pearls:
### A Faerie Strand
by Louise Hawes
(HMC, $16.00) 978-0-618-74797-9
Classical fairy tales have been transformed
and retold as sophisticated, complicated stories that don't always have a happy ending.
(12–14)

###  Eon:
### Dragoneye Reborn
by Alison Goodman
(Viking, $19.99) 978-0-670-06227-0
Eon's quest to become a powerful Dragoneye
is jeopardized by court politics, physical
injuries, and his hidden female identity.
(12–15)

### Guinevere's Gift
by Nancy McKenzie
(Knopf, $15.99) 978-0-375-84345-7
A courageous, rebellious girl later finds her
way to becoming King Arthur's queen.
(12–14)

### Impossible
by Nancy Werlin
(Dial, $17.99) 978-0-8037-3002-1
Can seventeen-year-old Lucy break the curse
that has driven generations of Scarborough
women into madness? (13–15)

### ★Nation
by Terry Pratchett
(HarperCollins, $17.89) 978-0-06-143302-3
When Mau's village is destroyed by the great
wave, he must determine for himself what it
means to be a man. (12–15)

James Stevenson 2008

### Sword
by Da Chen
(HarperCollins, $17.89) 978-0-06-144759-4
In ancient China, Miu employs wit and martial arts to avenge her father's murder.
(11–14)

### ★The Underneath
by Kathi Appelt, ill. by David Small
(Atheneum, $16.99) 978-1-4169-5058-5
Three interwoven stories about humans and
animals tell of loneliness, love, loyalty, and
danger. (11–15)

### The Unnameables
by Ellen Booraem
(Harcourt, $16.00) 978-0-15-206368-9
On an island where only useful objects are
named, a thirteen-year-old boy attempts to
bring change to a community. (14–16)

## HISTORICAL FICTION

### The Boy Who Dared:
### A Novel Based on the True
### Story of a Hitler Youth
by Susan Campbell Bartoletti
(Scholastic, $16.99) 978-0-439-68013-4
Helmut Huebner tells of his incarceration in
1942 for his attempt to tell the truth about
Hitler to the German people. (12–14)

## Brave Deeds: How One Family Saved Many from the Nazis
by Ann Alma
(Groundwood, $17.95) 978-0-88899-791-3
A fictional narrator relates the story of Frans and Mies Braal's bravery during the Dutch resistance of 1944–1945. Archival photographs. (12–14)

## ★Chains
by Laurie Halse Anderson
(S&S, $16.99) 978-1-4169-0585-1
During the Revolutionary War, a thirteen-year-old slave is sold to a cruel loyalist couple and must determine her own path to freedom. (12–14)

## Climbing the Stairs
by Padma Venkatraman
(Putnam, $16.99) 978-0-399-24746-0
A fifteen-year-old experiences the changes in India during World War II and the rise of Gandhi's non-violence movement. (12–15)

## Daughter of War
by Marsha Forchuk Skrypuch
(Fitzhenry & Whiteside, P$14.95)
978-1-55455-044-9
Marta and her sister survive the Armenian genocide and are reunited with Marta's betrothed. (11–14)

James Stevenson 2008

## ★The Diary of Laura's Twin
by Kathy Kacer
(Second Story Press, P$14.95)
978-1-897187-39-5
Although initially reluctant to participate in the Holocaust twinning project for her bat mitzvah, 12-year-old Laura becomes inspired and strengthened by it. (12–14)

## The Humming of Numbers
by Joni Sensel
(Henry Holt, $16.95) 978-0-8050-8327-9
Aiden, a monastic novice with mysterious numerical powers, joins Lara, the Lord's bastard, to battle raiding Vikings in twelfth-century Ireland. (12–14)

## I Am Apache
by Tanya Landman
(Candlewick, $17.99) 978-0-763-63664-7
A fourteen-year-old girl becomes a warrior to avenge her brother's death in this dramatic tale of the Apache Indians in the nineteenth century. (11–14)

## Ivy
by Julie Hearn
(Atheneum, $17.99) 978-1-4169-2506-4
A red-haired beauty from a family of thieves poses for a rich London artist in this Dickensian tale. (12–15)

## Jimmy's Stars
by Mary Ann Rodman
(FSG, $16.95) 978-0-374-33703-2
During World War II, sixth-grader Ellie experiences loss and sacrifice and grows emotionally. (10–13)

## Little Rock Nine
by Marshall Poe, ill. by Ellen Lindner
(Aladdin, P$7.99) 978-1-4169-5066-0
Two fictional students, one black, one white, participate in the historic struggle to integrate Central High in 1957 Arkansas. (12–14)

## ★Ⓜ On Beale Street
by Ronald Kidd
(S&S, $16.99) 978-1-4169-3387-8
Fifteen-year-old Johnny's life becomes complicated when he discovers Beale Street, music, the young Elvis, and the secrets in his own life. (13–14)

### The Red Necklace
by Sally Gardner
(Dial, $16.99) 978-0-8037-3100-4
A gypsy with magical powers rescues an innocent girl from the bloodshed of the French Revolution. (12–15)

### Ringside, 1925:
### Views from the Scopes Trial
by Jen Bryant
(Knopf, $15.99) 978-0-375-84047-0
The ways people disagreed about evolution in the past, and continue to do so today, are revealed in blank verse. (11–14)

### The Smile
by Donna Jo Napoli
(Dutton, $17.99) 978-0-525-47999-4
Through the eyes of teenage Elizabeth, we see Renaissance Florence and historical figures including Leonardo, Savonarola, and the Medicis. (12–15)

### The Walls of Cartagena
by Julia Durango, ill. by Tom Pohrt
(S&S, $15.99) 978-1-4169-4102-6
A boy in seventeenth-century Colombia rescues two slaves while interpreting for a priest and the doctor at a leper colony. (11–13)

### White Sands, Red Menace
by Ellen Klages
(Viking, $16.99) 978-0-670-06235-5
Dewey faces a difficult choice as the Gordon family struggles to stay together amid post-atomic-bomb politics in 1946 Almagordo, New Mexico. (12–15)

### The Winter War
by William Durbin
(Wendy Lamb, $15.99) 978-0-385-74652-6
In 1939, a young polio survivor, Marko, uses grit and skiing prowess to defend Finland against invading Russians. (12–14)

## SCIENCE FICTION

### ★ⓂThe Adoration
### of Jenna Fox
by Mary E. Pearson
(Henry Holt, $16.95) 978-0-8050-7668-4
Emerging from a year-long coma, seventeen-year-old Jenna learns that she has survived by illegal means. (11–16)

### ⓂThe Hunger Games
by Suzanne Collins
(Scholastic, $17.99) 978-0-439-02348-1
In a dystopic future, sixteen-year-old Katnis is selected to represent her impoverished district in events that require her to fight to the death. (12–16)

### The Other Side of the Island
by Allegra Goodman
(Penguin, $16.99) 978-1-59514-195-8
Honor and her family rebel to end the worldwide control of Earth Mother. (12–15)

### ▣Robert Louis Stevenson's
### Strange Case of
### Dr. Jekyll and Mr. Hyde
adapted by Alan Grant, ill. by Cam Kennedy
(Tundra, P$12.99) 978-0-88776-882-8
Appropriately dark and mysterious panels work well with the adapted text to introduce this classic. (12–14)

### Simon Bloom,
### The Gravity Keeper
by Michael Reisman
(Dutton, $15.99) 978-0-525-47922-2
Simon and two sixth-grade buddies apply a new discovery about the laws of physics as they battle evil forces in their town. (10–12)

## TODAY

### ★A Bottle in the Gaza Sea
by Valérie Zenatti
(Bloomsbury, $16.95) 978-1-59990-200-5
An Israeli girl sends a message across "enemy lines" and begins a powerful and unforgettable correspondence with a Palestinian boy. (12–14)

### Dreamrider
by Barry Jonsberg
(Knopf, $15.99) 978-0-375-84457-7
Teenager Michael Barry, bullied at school and at home because of his weight, uses his dreams to get revenge on his enemies. (12–14)

## Egghead

by Caroline Pignat
(Red Deer Press, P$11.95) 978-0-88995-399-4
What does a ninth grader do when her nerdy, longtime friend is the victim of sadistic bullies? (11–14)

## The House of Djinn

by Suzanne Fisher Staples
(FSG, $16.95) 978-0-374-39936-8
Fifteen-year-old Mumtaz and cousin Jameel are transformed by the customs and expectations of their Pakistani tribal leadership. Sequel to *Shabanu* and *Haveli*. (12–15)

## Looks

by Madeleine George
(Viking, $16.99) 978-0-670-06167-9
An anorexic poet and an obese loner join forces to survive and avenge high school betrayals. (12–14)

## Pain & Wastings

by Carrie Mac
(Orca, P$9.95) 978-1-55143-904-4
Living in a group home, Ethan meets a paramedic who is a link to his suppressed past. (12–14)

## ★Peeled

by Joan Bauer
(Putnam, $16.99) 978-0-399-23475-0
An upstate New York apple-growing community is threatened by double-dealing theme park developers and avaricious politicians until Hildy and her fellow reporters do an exposé. (12–14)

## Saturday Night Dirt

by Will Weaver
(FSG, $14.95) 978-0-374-35060-4
Car races draw drivers, fans, and workers who experience danger and romance in a small Minnesota town. (12–15)

## Season of Ice

by Diane Les Becquets
(Bloomsbury, $16.95) 978-1-59990-063-6
Gen is tough—racing cars in rural Maine—but when her father goes missing, she sets out to find him and herself. (12–14)

## ★Streams of Babel

by Carol Plum-Ucci
(Harcourt, $17.00) 978-0-15-216556-7
Brilliant teenage hackers oppose terrorists who attack an American town. (12–15)

## ★Sunrise Over Fallujah

by Walter Dean Myers
(Scholastic, $17.99) 978-0-439-91624-0
An eighteen-year-old from Harlem discovers the horrors of war during his service in Iraq. (12–15)

## The Writing on the Wall

by Wendy Lichtman
(Greenwillow, $16.99) 978-0-06-122958-9
Tess tests her math skills and moral principles to solve a school mystery. (11–14)

# FOURTEEN & UP

Harry Horse 1998

## Alicia Afterimage
by Lulu Delacre
(Lee & Low, $19.95) 978-1-60060-242-9
A grieving family and thirteen friends celebrate the life of a talented, beloved girl who was killed in a car accident. Included are resources for dealing with teen grief and driver safety.

## All We Know of Heaven
by Jacquelyn Mitchard
(HarperCollins, $16.99) 978-0-06-134578-4
When Maureen wakes from a coma, she is helped to recover by family and friends.

## Big Big Sky
by Kristyn Dunnion
(Red Deer Press, P$14.95) 978-0-88995-404-5
When a closely bonded female warrior group is recalled to the Living Lab for reprogramming, they escape into a surprising world.

## Bog Child
by Siobhan Dowd
(Random, $16.99) 978-0-385-75169-8
Eighteen-year-old Fergus is caught up in Ireland's troubles—both today and in the distant past.

## The Book of Jude
by Kimberley Heuston
(Front Street, $17.95) 978-1-932425-26-0
After being uprooted from New York, Jude struggles with emotional problems in 1989 Prague.

## Chandra's Wars
by Allan Stratton
(HarperCollins, $18.99) 978-0-06-087264-9
In Africa, teenager Chandra promised her dying mother that she would raise her younger siblings. Can she save them from becoming child soldiers?

## A Curse Dark as Gold
by Elizabeth C. Bunce
(Arthur A. Levine, $17.99) 978-0-439-89576-7
When a seventeen-year-old orphan tries to save her family's wool mill, the outlook is bleak, until the arrival of Jack Spinner.

## Feathered
by Laura Kasischke
(HarperCollins, $17.89) 978-0-06-081318-5
High school seniors Michelle and Anne experience Mayan ruins and their lives are changed forever.

## Forever Changes
by Brendan Halpin
(FSG, $16.95) 978-0-374-32436-0
Mathematically gifted, a high school senior with cystic fibrosis applies for MIT, fearing she'll never live long enough to attend.

## The Freedom Business
by Marilyn Nelson, ill. by Deborah Dancy
(Wordsong, $18.95) 978-1-932425-57-4
A poet responds to an eighteenth-century slave's moving autobiography of his journey to and life in America.

## Girl from Mars
by Tamara Bach, trans. by Shelley Tanaka
(Groundwood, $16.95) 978-0-88899-724-1
Bored with life in her small German town, fifteen-year-old Miriam finally finds love—with a girl.

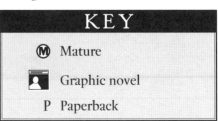

## KEY

Ⓜ Mature

👤 Graphic novel

P Paperback

### Graceling
by Kristin Cashore
(Harcourt, $17.00) 978-0-15-206396-2
Born with a special skill or Grace, Katsa is a feared killer until she finds the courage to rebel.

### Hidden Letters
annotated by Deborah Slier and Ian Shine, trans. by Marion van Binsbergen-Pritchard (Star Bright, $35.00) 978-1-887734-88-2
Teenager Flip Slier's letters from the Molengoot work camp in Holland during World War II are supplemented by annotations and essays giving the history of Dutch Jews' experiences during the Holocaust.

### How They Met, and Other Stories
by David Levithan
(Knopf, $16.99) 978-0-375-84886-5
Eighteen short stories describe teens and love in all its many variations.

### How to Build a House
by Dana Reinhardt
(Wendy Lamb, $15.99) 978-0-375-84453-9
Seventeen-year-old Harper escapes her family's turmoil by volunteering to help with construction in a tornado-devastated town.

### I Am Scout: The Biography of Harper Lee
by Charles J. Shields
(Henry Holt, $18.95) 978-0-8050-8334-7
A fascinating portrait of the unconventional and extremely private author of *To Kill a Mockingbird.*

### Identical
by Ellen Hopkins
(McElderry, $17.99) 978-1-4169-5005-9
Twin sixteen-year-old daughters of a judge and a congressional candidate struggle with secrets that have torn the family apart. Told in various verse forms.

### Lock and Key
by Sarah Dessen
(Viking, $18.99) 978-0-670-01088-2
Seventeen-year-old Ruby finds that she is not quite ready to become independent when her mother deserts her.

### Newes from the Dead
by Mary Hooper
(Roaring Brook, $16.95) 978-1-59643-355-7
The true story of Anne Green, hanged for infanticide in 1650, who lived to tell her story of betrayal.

### Pitch Black
ill. by Youme Landowne and Anthony Horton
(Cinco Puntos, $17.95) 978-1-933693-06-4
What's it like to be alone, homeless, and hungry? Two artists meet on a subway, forge a connection and find strength, dignity, and hope.

### Playing with Matches
by Brian Katcher
(Delacorte, $15.99) 978-0-385-73544-5
A seventeen-year-old debates whether to date the school beauty or the disfigured girl who shares all of his interests.

### Primavera
by Mary Jane Beaufrand
(Little, $16.99) 978-0-316-01644-5
Driven by greed, the Pazzi and the Medici engage in a bloody power struggle which leaves Flora Pazzi bereft of nearly everyone she loves.

### Saving Juliet
by Suzanne Selfors
(Walker, $16.95) 978-0-8027-9740-7
Mimi gets a chance to change the tragic ending of *Romeo and Juliet* when she is transported to Shakespeare's Verona.

### Skim
written by Mariko Tamaki, drawings by Jillian Tamaki
(Groundwood, $18.95) 978-0-88899-753-1
Suicide, depression, love, and finding a way to be your own "fully human self" are all observed and explored with compassion.

Harry Horse 1998

## Stealing Heaven
by Elizabeth Scott
(HarperCollins, $16.99) 978-0-06-112280-4
Danielle has been taught by her mother to
be a thief, but when she discovers friendship
and love, she begins to ask questions.

## Ⓜ Ten Mile River
by Paul Griffin
(Dial, $16.99) 978-0-8037-3284-1
Two homeless teenage boys find it hard to go
straight, even with the chance of a better life.

## Thaw
by Monica M. Roe
(Front Street, $17.95) 978-1-59078-496-9
Stricken with Guillain-Barré Syndrome,
Dane, a smart and superb skier, can't believe
that he doesn't control his own destiny.

## Three Little Words:
## A Memoir
by Ashley Rhodes-Courter
(Atheneum, $17.99) 978-1-4169-4806-3
Ashley is adopted after ten years in foster
homes and orphanages. The path from fear
of rejection to acceptance and love is often
painful.

## Trouble
by Gary D. Schmidt
(Clarion, $16.00) 978-0-618-92766-1
When a fatal accident occurs, a new
Cambodian community comes into conflict
with the traditional, nearby New England
town.

## Vidalia in Paris
by Sasha Watson
(Viking, $16.99) 978-0-670-01094-3
When Vidalia achieves her dream, a scholar-
ship to study art in Paris, she is introduced
to the beauty of the city but also faces many
moral choices.

## What They Always Tell Us
by Martin Wilson
(Delacorte, $15.99) 978-0-385-73507-0
Brothers Alex, seventeen, and James, a year
older, go through a very difficult year.

## Wish You Were Here
by Catherine Clark
(HarperCollins, $17.89) 978-0-06-055984-7
A quirky teenager's bus trip out West turns
into an unexpectedly interesting experience
for Ariel.

## Write Naked
by Peter Gould
(FSG, $16.95) 978-0-374-38483-8
In rural Vermont, sixteen-year-old Victor
and Rose Anna share a passion for nature
and writing.

# SPECIAL INTERESTS

Harry Horse 1998

## ACTIVITIES

### Can You See What I See? Nature
written and ill. by Walter Wick
(Scholastic, P$3.99) 978-0-439-86226-4
Young readers must locate hidden plants and animals and are introduced to simple nature vocabulary. (4–7)

### How to Speak Dog!
by Sarah Whitehead, photos by John Daniels
(Scholastic, P$6.99) 978-0-545-02078-7
Lively examples of how dogs communicate with humans and one another enhance this approach to training. (8–12)

### Paula Deen's My First Cookbook
by Paula Deen, with Martha Nesbit,
ill. by Susan Mitchell
(S&S, $21.99) 978-1-4169-5033-2
Each kid-friendly recipe illustrates the colorful ingredients and utensils required, followed by clear directions. Safety precautions and glossary included. (5–10)

### ★Yellow Square: A Pop-up Book for Children of All Ages
paper engineering by David Carter
(S&S, $23.99) 978-1-4169-4093-7
The artist uses his considerable skills to encourage children to find the yellow square. (4–7)

## ARTS

### ABCD
by Marion Bataille
(Roaring Brook, $19.95) 978-1-59643-425-7
Ingenious paper engineering illustrates the alphabet in black, red, and white. Full of surprises. (6–12)

### All Aboard!: A Traveling Alphabet
concept by Chris L. Demarest,
ill. by Bill Mayer
(McElderry, $17.99) 978-0-689-85249-7
Letters hide in many places as they journey around the world using different modes of transportation. (3–7)

### An Artist's America
by Michael Albert
(Henry Holt, $17.95) 978-0-8050-7857-2
The world of collage is presented with colorful, unique pieces by a modern Pop artist. (8–12)

### ★Before John Was a Jazz Giant: A Song of John Coltrane
by Carole Boston Weatherford,
ill. by Sean Qualls
(Henry Holt, $16.95) 978-0-8050-7994-4
A creative look at how the great musician transformed the many sounds he heard as a child into music. Acrylic, collage, and pencil illustrations. (6–9)

## KEY

★ Outstanding merit

 Read-aloud

. **SERIES TITLE**
| (series books follow)

**(4-6)** Age range

Ⓜ Mature

Ⓝ New edition

P Paperback

## Christo and Jeanne-Claude: Through the Gates and Beyond

by Jan Greenberg and Sandra Jordan
(Roaring Brook, $19.95) 978-1-59643-071-6
Engaging pictures and concise text give a glimpse into the lives, inspiration, and projects of Christo and his wife and collaborator. (10–14)

## Comic Book Century: The History of American Comic Books

by Stephen Krensky
(Twenty-First Century Books, $30.60)
978-0-8225-6654-0
The growth and changes of a popular art form are followed from Superman to graphic novels. Includes a select bibliography and website listing. (11–14)

## Lester Fizz, Bubble-Gum Artist

by Ruth Spiro, ill. by Thor Wickstrom
(Dutton, $16.99) 978-0-525-47861-4
Inspired by his artist family, Lester finds his own special talent. Humorous illustrations show noted artists' work. (7–10)

## Name That Style: All About Isms in Art

by Bob Raczka
(Millbrook, $25.26) 978-0-8225-7586-3
Naturalism, realism, cubism, impressionism, and more are explained with examples by famous artists. (9–14)

## Sandy's Circus: A Story About Alexander Calder

by Tanya Lee Stone, ill. by Boris Kulikov
(Viking, $16.99) 978-0-670-06268-3
The renowned sculptor created a famous animated circus of miniature figures from found materials such as wire and cork. Stylized, humorous illustrations. (5–8)

## Wham! The Art & Life of Roy Lichtenstein

by Susan Goldman Rubin
(Abrams, $18.95) 978-0-8109-9492-8
An account that traces the stylistic development of the industrious, inventive artist and explains his place in modern art. (11–14)

# BIOGRAPHY

## ★Abe's Honest Words: The Life of Abraham Lincoln

by Doreen Rappaport, ill. by Kadir Nelson
(Hyperion, $16.99) 978-142310408-7
Straightforward, poetic text and elegant, emotional paintings show the arc of Lincoln's lifelong quest to end slavery. (7–9)

## ★Amelia Earhart: The Legend of the Lost Aviator

by Shelley Tanaka, ill. by David Craig
(Abrams, $18.95) 978-0-8109-7095-3
Photographs and original artwork supplement the story of this famous pilot's life. (8–12)

## Art from Her Heart: Folk Artist Clementine Hunter

by Kathy Whitehead, ill. by Shane W. Evans
(Putnam, $16.99) 978-0-399-24219-9
An African-American laborer in Louisiana who became a folk artist depicts the hard life around her. Mixed-media illustrations include some of the artist's work. (7–10)

## Ballots for Belva: The True Story of a Woman's Race for the Presidency

by Sudipta Bardhan-Quallen,
ill. by Courtney A. Martin
(Abrams, $16.95) 978-0-8109-7110-3
Belva Lockwood struggled in her attempt to be the first woman candidate for president in 1884. Realistic illustrations. Includes glossary, bibliography, and timeline. (9–12)

## Barack Obama: Son of Promise, Child of Hope

by Nikki Grimes, ill. by Bryan Collier
(S&S, $16.99) 978-1-4169-7144-3
A young boy learns about Barack Obama's unique journey to adulthood. Realistic mixed-media illustrations. (6–9)

## ★Becoming Billie Holiday

by Carole Boston Weatherford,
ill. by Floyd Cooper
(Wordsong, $19.95) 978-1-59078-507-2
A powerful account of how Eleanor Fagan survived poverty, reform school, rape, and street life, and rose to become the legendary Billie Holiday. (13–15)

## Booker T. Washington: Teacher, Speaker, and Leader

by Suzanne Slade, ill. by Siri Weber Feeney
(Picture Window, $25.26)
978-1-4048-3977-9
The famous African-American educator who founded a school in Alabama had wide-ranging influence. Acrylic paintings and colored pencil illustrations. (7–9)

## A Caldecott Celebration: Seven Artists and Their Paths to the Caldecott Medal

by Leonard S. Marcus
(Walker, $19.95) 978-0-8027-9703-2
A tour of the studios of seven artists shows how and where they work. (8–12)

## Daniel Boone's Great Escape

by Michael P. Spradlin, ill. by Ard Hoyt
(Walker, $16.95) 978-0-8027-9581-6
The great frontiersman's capture by the Shawnee Indians in 1778 reveals his bravery and endurance. Dynamic watercolor and colored pencil illustrations. (8–12)

## Elizabeth Leads the Way: Elizabeth Cady Stanton and the Right to Vote

by Tanya Lee Stone, ill. by Rebecca Gibbon
(Henry Holt, $16.95) 978-0-8050-7903-6
The power of an astonishing woman had long-lasting ramifications for all Americans. Gouache and colored pencil illustrations. (7–10)

## ★Extraordinary Women from the Muslim World

by Natalie Maydell and Sep Riahi,
ill. by Heba Amin
(Global Content Ventures, $16.95)
978-0-9799901-0-6
An introduction to a select group of Muslim women from around the world and across the ages. (9–11)

## Fantastic Female Filmmakers

by Suzanne Simoni
(Second Story Press, P$10.95)
978-1-897187-36-4
Pioneering women wrestled with bears, took on Nazis, wrote about pineapple plantations, and took on other challenges. (9–14)

## George Washington Carver

by Tonya Bolden
(Abrams, $18.95) 978-0-8109-9366-2
This multi-talented African-American scientist transformed our understanding of caring for the earth and using its products. Archival photographs, bibliography. (8–11)

## Gerardus Mercator: Father of Modern Mapmaking

by Ann Heinrichs
(Compass Point, $23.95) 978-0-7565-3312-0
The fascinating origins of mapmaking, along with the life and times of a sixteenth-century cartographer, are described in detail. Archival illustrations, bibliography, and notes. (11–14)

## Helen Keller: The World in Her Heart

by Lesa Cline-Ransome, ill. by James Ransome
(HarperCollins, $16.99) 978-0-06-057074-3
Aided by her teacher, Anne Sullivan, Helen, blind and deaf, learns to use smell, touch, and taste and the skills of finger-spelling to interpret her world. Strong oil paintings. (6–8)

## ★Helen's Eyes: A Photobiography of Annie Sullivan, Helen Keller's Teacher

by Marfé Ferguson Delano
(National Geographic, $17.95)
978-1-4263-0209-1
Annie Sullivan was the teacher who opened up the world to Helen Keller. Archival photographs. (9–13)

## Hillary Rodham Clinton: Dreams Taking Flight

by Kathleen Krull, ill. by Amy June Bates
(S&S, $16.99) 978-1-4169-7129-0
Girls can aspire to do and be anything, even president of the United States. (6–9)

## Honda: The Boy Who Dreamed of Cars

by Mark Weston, ill. by Katie Yamasaki
(Lee & Low, $17.95) 978-1-60060-246-7
The admirable life of the master mechanic and inventor of motorcycles and cars is presented along with acrylic-on-canvas illustrations. (9–12)

### ★I, Matthew Henson: Polar Explorer

by Carole Boston Weatherford, ill. by Eric Velasquez
(Walker, $16.95) 978-0-8027–9688-2
The true story of the African-American explorer, one of the team which first reached the North Pole, is rendered in poetic text and stunning pastels. (6–9)

### Johnny Appleseed

by Jane Yolen, ill. by Jim Burke
(HarperCollins, $17.89) 978-0-06-059136-6
The combination of facts, legend, stories, poetry, and simple but powerful illustrations offers a colorful picture of Johnny's quirky life. (6–9)

### Lance in France

by Ashley MacEachern, ill. by Michelle Barbera
(HarperCollins, $16.99) 978-0-06-113192-9
The champion bike rider races to victory in the Tour de France. Colorful, action-packed illustrations. (3–7)

### ★Lincoln through the Lens: How Photography Revealed and Shaped an Extraordinary Life

by Martin W. Sandler
(Walker, $19.99) 978-0-8027-9666-0
At the dawn of photography, Lincoln learned to use the new medium while the world-shaking events of his times were recorded. (10–14)

Amy Wummer 2008

### ★The Lincolns: A Scrapbook Look at Abraham and Mary

by Candace Fleming
(S&W, $24.99) 978-0-375-83618-3
A fascinating collection of artifacts, anecdotal tales, and archival photographs follows the lives of this Civil War president and his wife. (11–15)

### Maggie L. Walker: Pioneering Banker and Community Leader

by Candice Ransom
(Twenty-First Century Books, $31.93) 978-0-8225-6611-3
The daughter of a freed slave, this determined woman worked a lifetime to ensure that African-American women would have equal footing with whites and men. (11–13)

### A Man for All Seasons: The Life of George Washington Carver

by Stephen Krensky, ill. by Wil Clay
(HarperCollins, $16.99) 978-0-06-027885-4
The difficulties, accomplishments, and influence of the famous African-American scientist are clearly described. Soft, realistic pastels. (9–11)

### ★Manjiro: The Boy Who Risked His Life for Two Countries

written and ill. by Emily Arnold McCully
(FSG, $16.95) 978-0-374-34792-5
A fourteen-year-old Japanese boy, rescued from a shipwreck, lives in America for many years before finding his way home. Detailed watercolors. (8–11)

### ★Marco Polo

written and ill. by Demi
(Cavendish, $19.99) 978-0-7614-5433-5
The exciting adventures of the great explorer and his family are accompanied by stylized illustrations. Detailed map references. (8–12)

## Mark Twain: An American Star

by Elizabeth MacLeod
(Kids Can, $14.95) 978-1-55337-908-9
The prolific author used humor to destroy barriers between the races. Illustrated with cartoons and photographs. (8–11)

## Nobel's Women of Peace

by Michelle Benjamin and Maggie Mooney
(Second Story, P$10.95)
978-1-897187-38-8
These women maintained their dignity, integrity, and principles while they fought for peace. (9–11)

## ★Piano Starts Here: The Young Art Tatum

written and ill. by Robert Andrew Parker
(S&W, $16.99) 978-0-375-83965-8
As the jazz pianist grows up, his great talent develops despite near blindness. Soft, expressive pen and watercolor illustrations. (7–10)

## The Road to Oz: Twists, Turns, Bumps, and Triumphs in the Life of L. Frank Baum

by Kathleen Krull, ill. by Kevin Hawkes
(Knopf, $17.99) 978-0-375-83216-1
The life of the creator of *The Wizard of Oz* reveals his long, difficult journey to success. Stylized India ink and acrylic illustrations. (9–12)

## Robert H. Jackson: New Deal Lawyer, Supreme Court Justice, Nuremberg Prosecutor

by Gail Jarrow
(Calkins Creek, $18.95) 978-1-59078-511-9
In his short life, Jackson played many roles and always stood for the rule of law. His judicial opinions are still relevant today. Timeline, notes, bibliography. (10–14)

## Seven Miles to Freedom: The Robert Smalls Story

by Janet Halfmann, ill. by Duane Smith
(Lee & Low, $17.95) 978-1-60060-232-0
Steering a Confederate gunboat into Union territory, Robert Smalls became a hero and one of the first African Americans to become a congressman. Expressive oil paintings. (7–10)

## ★She Touched the World: Laura Bridgman, Deaf-Blind Pioneer

by Sally Hobart Alexander and Robert Alexander
(Clarion, $18.00) 978-0-618-85299-4
The remakable woman who led the way for Helen Keller is given a special perspective by an author with some sight and hearing loss. (11–14)

## Stand Tall, Abe Lincoln

by Judith St. George, ill. by Matt Faulkner
(Philomel, $16.99) 978-0-399-24174-1
In his late childhood, Abe's life is changed by his new stepmother. Lively writing and comical gouache paintings. Bibliography. (7–10)

## ★The Trouble Begins at 8: A Life of Mark Twain in the Wild, Wild West

by Sid Fleischman
(Greenwillow, $18.99) 978-0-06-134431-2
Learn about Samuel Clemens's life as gold prospector, early standup comic, pilot, and writer in this carefully researched biography. (11–14)

James Stevenson 2008

· Up Close:

## W. E. B. DuBois
by Tonya Bolden

## Ella Fitzgerald
by Tanya Lee Stone

## Jane Goodall
by Sudipta Bardhan-Quallen

## Thurgood Marshall
by Chris Crowe

## Elvis Presley
by Wilborn Hampton

## John Steinbeck
by Milton Meltzer
(Viking, $16.99) 978-0-670-06139-6,
978-0-670-06149-5, 978-0-14-241148-3,
978-0-670-06263-8, 978-0-670-06228-7,
978-0-670-06302-4
This well-annotated series introduces many influential Americans. (9–14)

## Who Was Queen Elizabeth?
by June Eding, ill. by Nancy Harrison
(Penguin, $P4.99) 978-0-448-44839-8
In sixteenth-century England, Queen Elizabeth wielded great power over her people. An illustrated page-turner. (8–10)

## Women Daredevils: Thrills, Chills, and Frills
by Julie Cummins, ill. by Cheryl Harness
(Dutton, $17.99) 978-0-525-47948-2
Fourteen adventurous stunt women are profiled in these well-documented biographies. Poster-style illustrations. (9–12)

## ECOLOGY

## 10 Things I Can Do to Help My World: Fun and Easy Eco-Tips
written and ill. by Melanie Walsh
(Candlewick, $15.99) 978-0-7636-4144-3
Die-cut pages, clear text, and simple illustrations show children ways to care for the environment. (3–6)

## About Rodents: A Guide for Children
by Cathryn Sill, ill. by John Sill
(Peachtree, $15.95) 978-1-56145-454-9
Simple text and watercolors capture the habitats and diversity of rodents. Additional details at the back. (3–6)

## Generation Green: The Ultimate Teen Guide to Living an Eco-Friendly Life
by Linda Sivertsen and Tosh Sivertsen
(S&S, $P10.99) 978-1-4169-6122-2
Tips and facts on everything from a vegan diet to nail polish tell how everyone, including you, can make a difference. (10–13)

## Ⓝ I Wonder Why There's a Hole in the Sky and Other Questions About the Environment
by Sean Callery
(Kingfisher, $12.95) 978-0-7534-6249-2
The environmental relationships on earth are presented with hopeful ideas for protecting their delicate balance. (6–9)

## Ookpik: The Travels of a Snowy Owl
written and ill. by Bruce Hiscock
(Boyds Mills, $16.95) 978-1-59078-461-7
A young snowy owl travels farther south than usual. Impressionistic watercolors portray the changing landscape and open spaces. (5–8)

## To Be Like the Sun
by Susan Marie Swanson,
ill. by Margaret Chodos-Irvine
(Harcourt, $16.00) 978-0-15-205796-1
A little girl reflects on the stages of her sunflower's life from seed to towering plant. Bold color prints. (4–7)

## Wangari's Trees of Peace: A True Story from Africa
written and ill. by Jeanette Winter
(Harcourt, $17.00) 978-0-15-206545-4
A native of Kenya, Wangari shows the women of her town how to plant trees to restore the barren earth—and the movement spreads throughout Africa. Stylized acrylic illustrations. (5–8)

SPECIAL INTERESTS

## Wild Tracks!: A Guide to Nature's Footprints
written and ill. by Jim Arnosky
(Sterling, $14.95) 978-1-4027-3985-9
Actual-size footprints are represented, along with pencil and acrylic portraits of animals. (5–10)

## The Wolves Are Back
by Jean Craighead George,
paintings by Wendell Minor
(Dutton, $16.99) 978-0-525-47947-5
When the wolves returned to Yellowstone, they changed the landscape for the better, in just a few years. (5–8)

## All About Sleep: From A to ZZZZ
by Elaine Scott, illustrated by John O'Brien
(Viking, $17.99) 978-0-670-06188-4
Sleep, sleep disorders, dreams, and other sleep phenomena are clearly explained and accompanied by anecdotes and black-and-white drawings. (11–13)

## Bugs in My Hair?!
by Catherine Stier, ill. by Tammie Lyon
(Albert Whitman, $15.95) 978-0-8075-0908-1
Getting head lice is the worst thing Ellie can dream of until she is able to help others in her own special way. (5–9)

## The Tooth Book: A Guide to Healthy Teeth and Gums
written and ill. by Edward Miller
(Holiday House, $16.95) 978-0-8234-2092-6
This is a comprehensive, well-organized presentation of facts about teeth and tooth care. Bright, computer-generated illustrations. (4–8)

## Waiting for Benjamin: A Story about Autism
by Alexandra Jessup Altman,
ill. by Susan Keeter
(Albert Whitman, $15.95) 978-0-8075-7364-8
Alexander shares his story of how he learns to appreciate a brother with special needs. (5–9)

## ★Ain't Nothing But a Man: My Quest to Find the Real John Henry
by Scott Reynolds Nelson, with Marc Aronson
(National Geographic, $18.95)
978-1-4263-0000-4
Experience the process of scholarly discovery with this compelling account of historical research about the legendary "steel" driving man. (11–14)

## Ancient Celts: Archaeology Unlocks the Secrets of the Celts' Past
by Jen Green, Bettina Arnold, Consultant
(National Geographic, $17.95)
978-1-4263-0225-1
Archaeology reveals the widespread influence of the people who settled areas from the British Isles to the shores of the Black Sea. (12–14)

## Animals Robert Scott Saw: An Adventure in Antarctica
by Sandra Markle
(Chronicle, $16.99) 978-0-8118-4918-0
The natural history of Antarctica is depicted as part of the adventures and misadventures of early explorers. (7–10)

## Arab Science and Invention in the Golden Age
by Anne Blanchard, ill. by Emmanuel Cerisier
(Enchanted Lion, $19.95) 978-1-59270-080-6
The scientific discoveries during the Arab Golden Age are the focus of this absorbing history of the Muslims. Maps, time lines, glossary. (11–16)

## The Betrayal of Africa
by Gerald Caplan
(Groundwood, $18.95) 978-0-88899-824-8
This concise and beautifully annotated guide discusses the role of the West in creating the problems of contemporary Africa. (14–16)

## Building Manhattan
written and ill. by Laura Vila
(Viking, $16.99) 978-0-670-06284-3
A glimpse of Manhattan's birth and growth is enhanced by an elegantly simple text and vibrant, brightly colored illustrations. (5–7)

Nick Bruel 2008

## Colonial Voices: Hear Them Speak
by Kay Winters, ill. by Larry Day
(Dutton, $17.99) 978-0-525-47872-0
From the errand boy to the clockmaker, the people of Colonial America describe their times. Pen-and-ink and watercolor illustrations. (8–12)

## The Donkey of Gallipoli: A True Story of Courage in World War I
by Mark Greenwood, ill. by Frané Lessac
(Candlewick, $16.99) 978-0-7636-3913-6
Rich language and detailed gouache illustrations tell the story of a brave soldier and his donkey who rescued hundreds of wounded men. (8–10)

## Duel!: Burr and Hamilton's Deadly War of Words
by Dennis Brindell Fradin, ill. by Larry Day
(Walker, $16.95) 978-0-8027-9583-0
The tale of personal rivalry between two patriots that resulted in a death is accompanied by nuanced watercolors. (8–12)

## ★The Erie Canal
by Martha E. Kendall
(National Geographic, $18.95)
978-1-4263-0022-6
A riveting history of the "eighth" wonder of the world includes engaging cultural, political, and legal anecdotes. Archival illustrations. (11–13)

## Gay America: Struggle for Equality
by Linas Alsenas
(Amulet, $24.95)
978-0-8109-9487-4
How gay men and women have lived, worked, and loved since colonial times. (14–16)

## ★Heroes for Civil Rights
by David A. Adler, ill. by Bill Farnsworth
(Holiday House, $16.95) 978-0-8234-2008-7
'The Little Rock Nine,' Thurgood Marshall, Martin Luther King, Jr., and others involved in the Civil Rights movement are brought to life and illustrated with forceful oil paintings. Detailed timelines and bibliographies. (10–14)

## King George: What Was His Problem?: Everything Your Schoolbooks Didn't Tell You About the American Revolution
by Steve Sheinkin, ill. by Tim Robinson
(Roaring Brook, $19.95) 978-1-59643-319-9
This lively, anecdotal history of the American Revolution is accompanied by cartoon-like illustrations. Supplemental source material. (11–14)

## Ⓜ Kristallnacht, The Night of the Broken Glass: Igniting the Nazi War Against Jews
by Stephanie Fitzgerald
(Compass Point, $33.26) 978-0-7565-3489-9
A thorough and disturbing depiction illuminates the events in Germany leading to the Holocaust and World War II. (11–14)

## ★Lady Liberty: A Biography
by Doreen Rappaport, ill. by Matt Tavares
(Candlewick, $17.99) 978-0-7636-2530-6
The participants in the creation of the Statue of Liberty dramatically present their story. Vivid watercolor, ink, and pencil illustrations. (7–11)

## Mazes Around the World

by Mary D. Lankford, ill. by Karen Dugan
(HarperCollins, $17.89) 978-0-688-16520-8
A description of complex and puzzling creations around the world is accompanied by paintings and a map. (9–12)

## Our California/ Nuestra California

by Pam Muñoz Ryan, ill. by Rafael López,
Sp. trans. by Yanitzia Canetti
(Charlesbridge, $17.95) 978-1-58089-116-5/
978-1-58089-226-1
Vibrant, mural-style art and simple poems depict the history of the state. Spanish and English editions. (5–9)

## Pyramids and Mummies

by Anne Bolton
(S&S, $21.99) 978-1-4169-5873-4
Dive into the ancient world of Egyptian pharaohs and their practices surrounding death. Unusual triangular interactive format. (9–14)

## Real Pirates: The Untold Story of the Whydah from Slave Ship to Pirate Ship

by Barry Clifford, ill. by Gregory Manchess,
photos by Kenneth Garrett
(National Geographic, $16.95)
978-1-4263-0279-4
Sam Bellamy, famed pirate, and his treasure ship are brought to life through the hard work of an undersea archaeologist. (9–12)

## Ships: A Pop-Up Book

paper engineering by Robert Crowther
(Candlewick, $17.99) 978-0-7636-3852-8
The evolution of ships from early outriggers to supertankers is presented through ingenious paper engineering and detailed text. (10–14)

## Titanic: Disaster at Sea

by Martin Jenkins, ill. by Brian Sanders
(Candlewick, $12.99) 978-0-7636-3795-8
The fate of the Titanic is presented with photographs, clear illustrations, and accessible text. (9–12)

## Two Miserable Presidents: Everything Your Schoolbooks Didn't Tell You About the Civil War

by Steve Sheinkin, ill. by Tim Robinson
(Roaring Brook, $19.95) 978-1-59643-320-5
An engaging history of the United States Civil War is told with wacky quotes and wacky facts. (10–14)

## Voices from Colonial America: New France 1534-1763

by Richard Worth with José António Brandão
(National Geographic, $21.95)
978-1-4263-0147-6
Maps and archival illustrations bring to life this less familiar part of American history. (9–12)

## ★Washington at Valley Forge

by Russell Freedman
(Holiday House, $24.95) 978-0-8234-2069-8
A defining period during the U.S. Revolutionary War is vividly described. Archival photographs, bibliography, timeline, and citations included. (10–14)

## HOLIDAYS

## Bringing in the New Year

written and ill. by Grace Lin
(Knopf, $15.99) 978-0-375-83745-6
Vibrant illustrations bring to life the traditions and feelings of the Chinese New Year. (4–7)

## Celebrate Cinco de Mayo: with Fiestas, Music, and Dance

by Carolyn Otto
(National Geographic, $15.95)
978-1-4263-0215-2
Colorful photographs describe the history and celebration of this Mexican holiday. (5–7)

## Drummer Boy

written and ill. by Loren Long
(Philomel, $17.99) 978-0-399-25174-0
A beloved drummer boy endures a cold, lonely adventure until he is returned home in time to celebrate Christmas. Rich acrylic illustrations. (4–8)

### President's Day

by Anne Rockwell, pictures by Lizzy Rockwell
(HarperCollins, $17.89) 978-0-06-050195-2
Elementary school students put on a play
and share information about presidents and
elections. (4–7)

### Ten Little Christmas Presents

written and ill. by Jean Marzollo
(Scholastic, $9.99) 978-0-545-02791-5
A counting down book in which ten forest
animals find ten presents in the snow. Simple
rhymes and cheerful illustrations. (3–5)

### Thanksgiving: The True Story

by Penny Colman
(Henry Holt, $18.95) 978-0-8050-8229-6
An illustrated guide through the various ori-
gins, legends, and transformations of the
American Thanksgiving holiday. Archival
photographs. (10–13)

### 'Twas the Day Before Christmas: The Story of Clement Clarke Moore's Beloved Poem

by Brenda Seabrooke, ill. by Delana Bettoli
(Dutton, $16.99) 978-0-525-47816-4
Detailed period illustrations help explain the
writing of the classic poem. (5–8)

### LAW

### Declare Yourself: Speak. Connect. Act. Vote. More Than 50 Celebrated Americans Tell You Why

(Greenwillow, P$11.99) 978-0-06-147316-6
Some forget, others don't understand, and
many are too busy, but all eventually learn
why every vote counts. (11–14)

### ★No Choirboy: Murder, Violence, and Teenagers on Death Row

by Susan Kuklin
(Henry Holt, $17.95) 978-0-8050-7950-0
Young men tell the stories of how they got to
death row and why they're hopeful for the
future. (12–14)

### See How They Run: Campaign Dreams, Election Schemes, and the Race to the White House

by Susan E. Goodman, Elwood H. Smith
(Bloomsbury, P$9.95) 978-1-59990-171-8
Presidential campaigns throughout the history of the United States are described with
historical notes and simple explanations. List
of resources. (9–13)

### MATH

### Making Cents: The Nuts and Bolts of Money and a Whole Lot More!

by Elizabeth Keeler Robinson,
ill. by Bob McMahon
(Tricycle, $14.95) 978-1-58246-214-1
In this creative introduction to United States
currency, kids work hard to earn enough
money to build a clubhouse. (6–10)

### Sort It Out!

by Barbara Mariconda, ill. by Sherry Rogers
(Sylvan Dell, $16.95) 978-1-934359-11-2
Pack Rat discovers the many ways of sorting
his found objects, but is surprised when
some of them disappear. Endearing illustrations. (5–7)

### MEMOIR

### The Bat-Chen Diaries

by Bat-Chen Shahak
(Kar-Ben, $7.95) 978-0-8225-7223-7
Family, friendship, and peace are among the
concerns in the poetic writings of an Israeli
girl who was killed by terrorists in 1996 at
age fifteen. (12–15)

### ★How I Learned Geography

written and ill. by Uri Shulevitz
(FSG, $16.95) 978-0-374-33499-4
A child who lives in the face of hardship
experiences the tremendous power of imagining a larger world. Pen-and-ink and watercolor illustrations. (5–8)

## ★Knucklehead: Tall Tales & Mostly True Stories About Growing Up Scieszka

by Jon Scieszka
(Viking, $16.99) 978-0-670-01106-3
This hilarious account of growing up with five brothers in the '50s and '60s is complete with references to bodily functions and epic tales of pranks and sibling rivalry. (8–12)

## Mao's Last Dancer: Young Reader's Edition

by Li Cunxin
(Walker, $16.99) 978-0-8027-9779-7
Determination takes a peasant from Mao's China to the Beijing Dance Company and to stardom in the Houston Ballet. (12–14)

## Snow Falling in Spring: Coming of Age in China during the Cultural Revolution

by Moying Li, calligraphy by Gao Xiang
(FSG, $16.00) 978-0-374-39922-1
Sheltered by her loving and educated family, the author finds her life turned upside down at age twelve by the Cultural Revolution. (12–15)

## Students on Strike: Jim Crow, Civil Rights, Brown, and Me

by John A. Stokes, with Lois Wolfe and Herman J. Viola
(National Geographic, $15.95)
978-1-4263-0153-7
In 1951, students at a high school in rural Virginia go on strike to protest their separate but unequal education. (12–14)

## I Get So Hungry

by Bebe Moore Campbell, ill. by Amy Bates
(Putnam, $16.99) 978-0-399-24311-0
Young Nikki finds the courage to improve her health with the companionship and inspiration of her teacher. (8–11)

## Mother's Song: A Lullaby

adapted by Ellin Greene,
ill. by Elizabeth Sayles
(Clarion, $17.00) 978-0-395-71527-7
A tender rhapsody of a mother's love, as adapted from a traditional English lullaby. Sensitive pastel illustrations. (3–5)

## Punk Wig

by Lori Ries, ill. by Erin Eitter Kono
(Boyds Mills, $16.95) 978-1-59078-486-0
When she loses her hair because of chemotherapy, Mom gets an orange punk wig. Cheerful watercolors provide some levity. (6–8)

## Barefoot: Poems for Naked Feet

by Stefi Weisburd,
ill. by Lori McElrath-Eslick
(Wordsong, $16.95) 978-1-59078-306-1
Twenty-seven poems muse on the beauty, fun, and freedom of being barefoot. (5–8)

## Birds on a Wire

by J. Patrick Lewis and Paul B. Janeczko,
ill. by Gary Lippincott
(Wordsong, $17.95) 978-1-59078-383-2
A walk around town in an American village is told in renga, an old Japanese verse form for two voices. Detailed watercolors. (5–8)

## ★The Blacker the Berry

by Joyce Carol Thomas, ill. by Floyd Cooper
(HarperCollins, $16.99) 978-0-06-025375-2
Poems celebrate the wonder of our diversity with soft, expressive illustrations. (4–10)

## Colors! Colores!

by Jorge Luján, ill. by Piet Grobler
(Groundwood, $17.95) 978-0-88899-863-7
In English and Spanish, these poems give gentle fleeting glimpses of shades of colors in natural settings. Sensitive watercolors. (6–10)

## Come and Play: Children of Our World Having Fun: Poems by Children

edited by Ayana Lowe
(Bloomsbury, $16.95) 978-1-59990-245-6
Superb photographs of children at play around the world accompany poems by children. (4–10)

## ★Frida: Viva la Vida! Long Live Life!

by Carmen T. Bernier-Grand,
ill. by Frida Kahlo
(Cavendish, $18.99) 978-0-7614-5336-9
Emotional poems, along with Kahlo's paintings, bring this intense artist to life. (10–14)

## Hip Hop Speaks to Children: A Celebration of Poetry with a Beat

edited by Nikki Giovanni
(Sourcebooks, $19.99) 978-1-4022-1048-8
Rhythmic verse by a variety of poets, including Langston Hughes, Lucille Clifton, Queen Latifah, and the Sugar Hill Gang, is accompanied by an audio CD and bold colorful illustrations. (7–10)

## ★Imaginary Menagerie: A Book of Curious Creatures

by Julie Larios, ill. by Julie Paschkis
(Harcourt, $16.00) 978-0-15-206325-2
Clever poems and stylized gouache illustrations give an imaginative, mythological view of many cultures and peoples. (6–9)

## ★Keepers: Treasure-Hunt Poems

by John Frank, photos by Ken Robbins
(Roaring Brook, $17.95) 978-1-59643-197-3
Found objects such as shells from the beach, baseball cards from the attic, and comics from a flea market provide inspiration for concise lyrical poems. (6–10)

## ★Keeping the Night Watch

by Hope Anita Smith, ill. by E.B. Lewis
(Henry Holt, $18.95) 978-0-8050-7202-0
The impact on a thirteen-year-old of a father's return to the family is revealed in powerful poetry. Realistic, soft brush illustrations. (9–13)

## M is for Mischief: An A to Z of Naughty Children

by Linda Ashman, ill. by Nancy Carpenter
(Dutton, $16.99) 978-0-525-47564-4
In this witty wordplay collection, children get their comeuppance for bad behavior. Humorous, energetic collages. (6–9)

## My Dog May Be a Genius

by Jack Prelutsky, ill. by James Stevenson
(Greenwillow, $19.89) 978-0-06-623863-0
The first Poet Laureate of Children's Literature presents a new collection of clever, funny poems. Black-and-white pen-and-ink drawings. (8–11)

## My Letter to the World and Other Poems

by Emily Dickinson,
ill. by Isabelle Arsenault
(Kids Can, $17.95) 978-1-55453-103-5
Some of Emily Dickinson's best known poems are sensitively illustrated in mixed media. (12–15)

## Pizza, Pigs, and Poetry: How to Write a Poem

by Jack Prelutsky
(Greenwillow, $16.99) 978-0-06-143449-5
Insights on how to create a poem are given along with examples, a glossary, and illustrations. (8–14)

## School Fever

by Brod Bagert, ill. by Robert Neubecker
(Dial, $16.99) 978-0-8037-3201-8
A child's offbeat view of school life. Bold, humorous artwork. (6–9)

## Shoe Bop!

by Marilyn Singer, ill. by Hiroe Nakata
(Dutton, $15.99) 978-0-525-47939-0
Choosing a new pair of shoes is a daunting, but exciting experience for a young girl. Colorful, bouncy illustrations. (4–7)

Nick Bruel 2008

## Side by Side: New Poems Inspired by Art from Around the World

edited by Jan Greenberg
(Abrams, $19.95) 978-0-8109-9471-3
Poems from around the world in the original language and in English translation accompany works of art. Reproductions and biographies of both poets and artists. Index and maps. (13–15)

## ★The Surrender Tree: Poems of Cuba's Struggle for Freedom

by Margarita Engle
(Henry Holt, $16.95) 978-0-8050-8674-4
Slaves, their hunters, and a legendary healer give voice to the horrors of war and the determination of Cubans to gain their independence. (12–14)

## ★Wabi Sabi

by Mark Reibstein, ill. by Ed Young
(Little, $16.99) 978-0-316-11825-5
A Japanese cat sets out to learn the meaning of her name in this blend of collage, prose, and haiku. (8–12)

## REFERENCE

### Children of the U.S.A.

by Maya Ajmera, et al.
(Charlesbridge, $23.95) 978-1-57091-615-1
Children travel through the fifty states celebrating diversity, learning, and the arts. Exuberant photographs. (7–10)

### L Is for LollyGag: Quirky Words for a Clever Tongue

by Molly Glover, ill. by Melinda Beck
(Chronicle, $12.99) 978-0-8118-6021-5
Discover oodles of quirky, vivid, and useful words. (10–14)

## T is for Tugboat: Navigating the Seas from A to Z

by Shoshanna Kirk
(Chronicle, $15.99) 978-0-8118-6094-9
This alphabet book with a nautical theme, vintage illustrations, and contemporary photographs is fascinating and encyclopedic. (6–10)

### Totally Tolerant: Spotting and Stopping Prejudice

by Diane Webber and Laurie Mandel
(Scholastic, $8.95) 978-0-531-13867-0
Clear information about prejudice and how to combat it is presented in this accessible guide. (10–13)

### United Tweets of America

written and ill. by Hudson Talbott
(Putnam, $17.99) 978-0-399-24520-6
Countless fun facts and irreverent humor fill this illustrated guide to the birds of our fifty states. (10–12)

## SCIENCE

### 11 Planets: A New View of the Solar System

written and ill. by David A. Aguilar
(National Geographic, $16.95)
978-1-4263-0236-7
This new view of the solar system includes the re-classification of the planets—terrestrial, giants, and dwarfs. Clear, labeled illustrations. (9–12)

### American Alligators: Freshwater Survivors

by Aaron Feigenbaum
(Bearport, $25.27) 978-1-59716-503-7
Colorful photographs and clearly written text convey information about the near extinction and recovery of these reptiles. (7–9)

### Animal Tracks & Signs

by Jinny Johnson
(National Geographic, $24.95)
978-1-4263-0253-4
Learn how to identify mammal, reptile, bird, and invertebrate tracks in your own backyard and around the world. (10–14)

Nick Bruel 2008

Nick Bruel 2008

## ★Bees, Snails, & Peacock Tails

by Betsy Franco, ill. by Steve Jenkins
(McElderry, $16.99) 978-1-4169-0386-4
Shapes, colors, and patterns in nature are
explored through poetic text and dynamic
collages. (4–8)

## The Best Book of the Human Body

by Barbara Taylor
(Kingfisher, $12.95) 978-0-7534-6031-3
Detailed diagrams and simple text explain
how the various parts of the body work.
Photographs and helpful illustrations.
Includes glossary. (7–9)

## Breakfast in the Rainforest: A Visit with Mountain Gorillas

written and photographed by Richard Sobel
(Candlewick, $18.99) 978-0-7636-2281-7
A photographer visits the endangered goril-
las in the African rainforest. Outstanding
photos. (9–12)

## Dazzling Dragonflies: A Life Cycle Story

by Linda Glaser, ill. by Mia Posada
(Millbrook, $22.60) 978-0-8225-6753-0
The life cycle of this fascinating creature is
presented with realistic watercolors. (5–7)

## Dinosaurs

by Judy Allen and Tudor Humphries
(Kingfisher, $7.95) 978-0-7534-6221-8
Questions about how they lived and what
happened to them are answered with helpful
illustrations and a pronunciation guide. (6–8)

## Face to Face with Frogs

written and photographed by
Mark W. Moffett

## Face to Face with Cheetahs

written and photographed by Chris Johns,
with Elizabeth Carney

## Face to Face with Lions

written and photographed by
Beverly Joubert and Dereck Joubert
(National Geographic, $16.95)
978-1-4263-0205-3, 978-1-4263-0323-4,
978-1-4263-0207-7
Creatures from around the world are
described clearly along with vivid
photographs. (7–10)

## Finding Home

by Sandra Markle, ill. by Alan Marks
(Charlesbridge, $15.95) 978-1-58089-122-6
A koala's courageous search for food and
shelter is based on the real-life story of a
koala nicknamed Cinders. Realistic watercolor, pen, and pencil illustrations. (7–10)

## Hide and Seek: Nature's Best Vanishing Acts

by Andrea Helman, photos by Gavriel Jecan
(Walker, $16.95) 978-0-8027-9690-5
The search for hidden creatures in their
diverse environments is accompanied by
sharp color photographs. Additional facts
included. (4–8)

## Horse

by Malachy Doyle, ill. by Angelo Rinaldi
(McElderry, $16.99) 978-1-4169-2467-8
The simple story of a foal's growth into a
horse is depicted with lush oil paintings.
(5–8)

## Human Body

by Linda Calabresi
(S&S, $16.99) 978-1-4169-3861-3
The state-of-the-art multi-dimensional perspective makes the subject matter accessible
and stimulating. (9–13)

Nick Bruel 2008

SPECIAL INTERESTS

## Hurricane!
written and ill. by Celia Godkin
(Fitzhenry & Whiteside, $19.95)
978-1-55455-080-7
The way animals, humans, and the land
survive after a hurricane is described with
clarity and mood-setting mixed-media
illustrations. (8–11)

### • INSECT WORLD

## Hornets:
**Incredible Insect Architects**
## Luna Moths:
**Masters of Change**
## Termites:
**Hardworking Insect Families**
by Sandra Markle
(Lerner, $27.93) 978-0-8225-7297-8,
978-0-8225-7302-9, 978-0-8225-7301-2
Life cycles are told in detail with dramatic
photographs. (9–12)

## Insects & Spiders
by Noel Tait
(S&S, $16.99) 978-1-4169-3868-2
This well-illustrated and documented
description of these creatures is clear and
accessible. (10–14)

## Life on Earth—and Beyond:
An Astrobiologist's Quest
by Pamela S. Turner
(Charlesbridge, $19.95) 978-1-58089-133-2
Extremely dry, hot, and cold places may hold
the key to life on Mars. (10–14)

## Look Behind!:
Tales of Animal Ends
by Lola M. Schaefer and Heather Lynn Miller,
ill. by Jane Manning
(Greenwillow, $17.89) 978-0-06-088394-2
Fascinating animal facts about the rear ends
of a variety of animals are presented in an A
to Z format. Wacky watercolor illustrations.
(7–9)

### • LOOKING CLOSELY

## Looking Closely
Along the Shore
## Looking Closely
Through the Forest
written and photographed by
Frank Serafini
(Kids Can, $15.95) 978-1-55453-141-7,
978-1-55453-212-4
Exquisite photography brings to life the
smallest wonders of these natural habitats.
(3–6)

### • MICROQUESTS

## Mighty Animal Cells
## Ultra-Organized Cell Systems
by Rebecca L. Johnson,
ill. by Jack Desrocher,
diagrams by Jennifer E. Fairman, CMI
(Millbrook, $29.27) 978-0-8225–7137-7,
978-0-8225–7138-4
The many diagrams, illustrations, and photographs of cells illuminate their uses in
various organisms. (9–11)

## The Mysterious Universe:
Supernovae, Dark Energy,
and Black Holes
text by Ellen Jackson,
photographs and illustrations by Nic Bishop
(HMC, $18.00) 978-0-618-56325–8
A team of astronomers searches for supernovae and explores the galaxies in our
universe. Well referenced with vivid
photography. (10–14)

## ★Nic Bishop Frogs
written and photographed by Nic Bishop
(Scholastic, $17.99) 978-0-439-87755–8
A description of the many varieties of this
amphibian is accompanied by brilliant color
photographs. (6–10)

Nick Bruel 2008

## · NO BACKBONE! THE WORLD OF INVERTEBRATES

### Deadly Praying Mantises
by Meish Goldish

### Prickly Sea Stars
by Natalie Lunis

### Smelly Stink Bugs
by Meish Goldish,
consultant Brian V. Brown
(Bearport Publishing, $21.28)
978-1-59716-582-2, 978-1-59716-508-2,
978-1-59716-580-8
These accessible, fully illustrated guides
illuminate the invertebrate world for young
readers. Enlarged photographs. (5–8)

### Oscar and the Bat: A Book About Sound
written and ill. by Geoff Waring
(Candlewick, $14.99) 978-0-7636-4025-5
A cat and a bat explore the concept of
sound. Vibrant, digitally rendered
illustrations. (6–8)

### Outbreak: Science Seeks Safeguards for Global Health
by Charles Piddock
(National Geographic, $17.95)
978-1-4263-0357-9
Photographs, diagrams, and maps enhance
the detailed description of epidemics and
what science is doing to control them.
(12–16)

### ★Pale Male: Citizen Hawk of New York City
by Janet Schulman, ill. by Meilo So
(Knopf, $16.99) 978-0-375-84558-1
New Yorkers come to the rescue of a red-tail
hawk family when they are threatened with
eviction. Cityscapes in watercolors. (7–11)

### Please Don't Wake the Animals: A Book About Sleep
by Mary Batten, ill. by Higgins Bond
(Peachtree, $16.95) 978-1-56145-393-1
Fascinating facts about the different sleep
patterns of a wide variety of species are
accompanied by realistic acrylic illustrations.
(6–10)

### Saving the Whooping Crane
by Susan E. Goodman, ill. by Phyllis V. Saroff
(Millbrook, $25.26) 978-0-8225-6748-6
A fascinating tale tells how scientists taught a
group of whooping cranes to fly a new east-
ern route, rescuing them from extinction.
(8–10)

### Seeing Red: The Planet Mars
by Nancy Loewen, ill. by Jeff Yesh
(Picture Window, $25.26) 978-1-4048-3953-3
Mars's size, orbit, temperature, and other
facts are presented clearly with digitally rendered illustrations. (7–9)

### Sisters & Brothers: Sibling Relationships in the Animal World
by Steve Jenkins and Robin Page,
ill. by Steve Jenkins
(HMC, $16.00) 978-0-618-37596-7
From helping to competing, siblings of the
animal world display a diversity of styles.
(5–9)

### Southern Sea Otters: Fur-tastrophe Avoided
by Jeanette Leardi
(Bearport, $25.27) 978-1-59716-534-1
Dedicated environmentalists value, care for,
and advocate for sea otters in an effort to
improve their endangered status. Vivid
photographs. (7–10)

### Sparrows
by Hans Post and Kees Heij,
ill. by Irene Goede
(Boyds Mills, $16.95) 978-1-59078-570-6
Realistic illustrations bring to life the world
of the oft-ignored house sparrow. (4–8)

### The Story of Science: Einstein Adds a New Dimension
by Joy Hakim
(Smithsonian, $27.95) 978-1-58834-162-4
A clear, engrossing narrative of the discoveries in physics from Copernicus to nuclear
physics. Illuminating charts, maps, and
diagrams. (12–15)

### ★Termites on a Stick: A Chimp Learns to Use a Tool
written and ill. by Michele Coxon
(Star Bright, $17.95) 978-1-59572-121-1
A mother teaches her child a basic survival skill, that of food gathering. Finely detailed illustrations along with additional information. (4–8)

### ★The Way We Work: Getting to Know the Amazing Human Body
written and ill. by David Macaulay
(HMC, $35.00) 978-0-618-23378-6
Both humorous and revealing, Macaulay's clear text and distinctive illustrations shed light on a complex subject. (12–14)

### A Wombat's World
written and ill. by Caroline Arnold
(Picture Window, $26.60) 978-1-4048-3986-1
Simple text and intricate cut-paper illustrations capture the life of this interesting Australian marsupial. (5–7)

### Your Skin Holds You In
by Becky Baines
(National Geographic, $14.95)
978-1-4263-0311-1
The various functions of this bodily organ that stretches, repairs itself, and prevents disease are described. References included. (4–7)

## SPORTS

### En Garde!: A Girl's Introduction to the World of Fencing
by Carlos Velez III, photos by Alex J. Ripa and Carlos Velez III
(Wish Publishing, P$16.95) 978-1930546899
Swordfighting, ballet, chess, and martial arts combine to create the challenging, athletically demanding, and magical world of fencing. (11–14)

### ★We Are the Ship: The Story of Negro League Baseball
written and ill. by Kadir Nelson
(Jump at the Sun, $18.99) 978-07860832-8
The hardships and triumphs of talented players, many of whom were kept from the major leagues because of color. Brilliant paintings. (10–14)

## WORLD

### Afghan Dreams: Young Voices of Afghanistan
by Tony O'Brien and Mike Sullivan, photos by Tony O'Brien
(Bloomsbury, $18.99) 978-1-59990-287-6
Magnificent photographic portraits of Afghani young people accompany their thoughts about their lives and their futures. (8–12)

### Horse Song: The Naadam of Mongolia
by Ted Lewin and Betsy Lewin
(Lee & Low, $19.95) 978-1-58430-277-3
We join a family of horse trainers, where nine-year-old Tomin will race a half-wild horse in the ancient desert race. Reed pen and watercolor illustrations. (8–12)

### One Peace: True Stories of Young Activists
written and ill. by Janet Wilson
(Orca, $19.95) 978-1-55143-892-4
This international anthology of stories about child activists for peace includes photos and poetry. Inspiring! (8–14)

### ★Show Me the Money: How to Make Cents of Economics
by Alvin Hall
(DK, $15.99) 978-0-7566-3762-0
Everything you want to know about economics is clearly explained and peppered with humor. (11–16)

## To Grandmother's House: A Visit to Old-Town Beijing

written and photographed by
Douglas Keister
(Gibbs Smith, $15.95) 978-1-4236-0283-5
On the way to visit their grandmother, cousins give a tour in pictures of her Beijing neighborhood. English and Mandarin. (6–8)

## Unsettled: The Problem of Loving Israel

by Marc Aronson
(Atheneum, $18.99) 978-1-4169-1261-3
Many complex issues are addressed in this thoughtful and provocative account of the history of Israel and the Palestinian-Israeli conflict. Maps and photos. (12–16)

## Voices in First Person: Reflections on Latino Identity

edited by Lori Marie Carlson,
photos by Manuel Rivera-Ortiz
(Atheneum, $16.99) 978-1-4169-0635-3
Diverse first-person vignettes describe the authors' feelings about life in America. (12–14)

## ★What the World Eats

by Faith D'Aluisio, photos by Peter Menzel
(Tricycle, $22.99) 978-1-58246-246-2
Everybody eats—but what? How much? 25 families from 21 different countries get and prepare their food. Magnificent photographs. (10–16)

# THE BEST BOOKS OF THE CENTURY

In 2009 we celebrate the 100th anniversary of the Children's Book Committee. What follows is a representative sampling of the best children's books of the year from the many, many titles that the committee has recommended from over a century of reading. These books reflect the goals and values of the Children's Book Committee through the decades. While many of the titles will be familiar, we have tried to emphasize books that we think may be missed by readers more often than the "obvious" classics—for example *The Enchanted Castle* rather than *Mother Goose*. We hope readers will find this list both useful and enlightening.

**1900-1920s:**

*Anne of Green Gables* by Lucy Maud Montgomery (9–11)

*The Enchanted Castle* by Edith Nesbit (9–11)

*Millions of Cats* written and ill. by Wanda Gág (5-7)

*Peter Pan* by James M. Barrie (10–12)

*Rebecca of Sunnybrook Farm* by Kate Douglas Wiggin (9–11)

*The Secret Garden* by Frances Hodgson Burnett (8–12)

*The Tale of Peter Rabbit* written and ill. by Beatrix Potter (5-7)

*The Velveteen Rabbit* by Margery Williams (4-6)

*The Wind in the Willows* by Kenneth Grahame (8–12)

*Winnie-the-Pooh* by A. A. Milne, ill. by Ernest Shepard (5-7)

*The Wonderful Wizard of Oz* by L. Frank Baum, ill. by W. W. Denslow (8–12)

**1930s:**

*The ABC Bunny* written and ill. by Wanda Gág (3-5)

*Andy and the Lion* written and ill. by James Daugherty (5-7)

*The Hobbit; or, There and Back Again* by J. R. R. Tolkien (9 and up)

*The Little Engine That Could* by Watty Piper, ill. by Lois Lenski (3-5)

*Mary Poppins* by P. L. Travers, ill. by Mary Shepard (9–11)

*National Velvet* by Enid Bagnold (10 and up)

*The Story of Ferdinand* written by Munro Leaf, ill. by Robert Lawson (5-7)

## 1940s:

*Betsy and Joe* by Maud Hart Lovelace (12 and up)

*Call Me Charley* by Jesse Jackson, ill. by Doris Spiegel (10-12)

*Caps for Sale* written and ill. by Esphyr Slobodkina (5-7)

*The Carrot Seed* written by Ruth Krauss, ill. by Crockett Johnson (5-7)

*Curious George* written and ill. by H. A. Rey (5-7)

*Eddie and the Fire Engine* written and ill. by Carolyn Haywood (8-10)

*The Fabulous Flight* written and ill. by Robert Lawson (9-11)

*Goodnight Moon* by Margaret Wise Brown, ill. by Clement Hurd (2-4)

*The Hundred Dresses* by Eleanor Estes, ill. by Louis Slobodkin (10-12)

*The Little Golden Book of Poetry* ill. by Corinne Malvern (5-7)

*The Little House* written and ill. by Virginia Lee Burton (5-7)

*Little Town on the Prairie* by Laura Ingalls Wilder, ill. by Helen Sewell and Mildred Boyle (8-10)

*Make Way for Ducklings* written and ill. by Robert McCloskey (2-3)

*Strawberry Girl* written and ill. by Lois Lenski (10-12)

*The Story of Babar* written and ill. by Jean de Brunhoff (2-3)

*Tim to the Rescue* by Edward Ardizzone (5-7)

*The Twenty-One Balloons* by William Pene du Bois (10-12)

*White Snow, Bright Snow* by Alvin Tresselt, ill. by Roger Duvoisin (2-4)

## 1950s:

*All-of-a-Kind Family* by Sydney Taylor, ill. Helen John Follet (9-11)

*And Now, Miguel* by Joseph Krumgold (9-11)

*Anne Frank: The Diary of a Young Girl* by Anne Frank (12 and up)

*The Borrowers* by Mary Norton (9-11)

*Bronxville Boys and Girls* by Gwendolyn Brooks, ill. by Ronni Solbert (7-9)

*The Cat in the Hat* written and ill. by Dr. Seuss (5-7)

*Charlottte's Web* by E. B. White, ill. by Garth Williams (9-11)

*Crictor* written and ill. by Tomi Ungerer (5-7)

*Crow Boy* written and ill. by Taro Yashima (5-7)

*Danny and the Dinosaur* written and ill. by Syd Hoff (5-7)

*Emmett's Pig* by Mary Stolz, ill. by Garth Williams (5-7)

*Harold and the Purple Crayon* written and ill. by Crockett Johnson (5-7)

*Harry the Dirty Dog* by Gene Zion, ill. by Mary Bloy Graham (5-7)

*Henry Huggins* by Beverly Cleary, ill. by Louis Darling (7-9)

*A Hole Is to Dig* by Ruth Krauss, ill. Maurice Sendak (2-4)

*The House of Sixty Fathers* by Meindert DeJong (13 and over)

*Little Bear* by Else Holmelund Minarik, ill. by Maurice Sendak (5-7)

*The Lion, the Witch and the Wardrobe* by C. S. Lewis, ill. by Pauline Baynes (9-11)

*Madeline's Rescue* written and ill. by Ludwig Bemelmans (5-7)

*Pippi Longstocking* by Astrid Lindgren, ill. by Louis Glanzman (7-9)

*The Rabbits' Wedding* written and ill. by Garth Williams (5-7)

**1960s:**
*About The B'nai Bagels* written and ill. by E. L. Konigsburg (10-12)

*Amelia Bedelia and the Surprise Shower* by Peggy Parish, ill. by Fritz Siebel (5-7)

*A Bear Called Paddington* by Michael Bond, ill. by Peggy Fortnum (7-9)

*Bedtime for Frances* by Russell Hoban, ill. by Garth Williams (3-5)

*The Case of the Hungry Stranger* written and ill. by Crosby Bonsall (5-7)

*The Cay* by Theodore Taylor (11-13)

*The Contender* by Robert Lipsyte (12-14)

*Corduroy* written and ill. by Don Freeman (3-5)

*The Cricket in Times Square* by George Selden, ill. by Garth Williams (9 and up)

*Encyclopedia Brown* by Donald J. Sobol, ill. by Leonard Shortall (7-9)

*The Ghost in the Noonday Sun* by Sid Fleischman, ill. by Warren Chappell (9-11)

*The Giving Tree* written and ill. by Shel Silverstein (5-8)

*Harriet the Spy* by Louise Fitzhugh (10-12)

*The High King* by Lloyd Alexander (11-13)

*I Am the Darker Brother* edited by Arnold Adoff, ill. by Benny Andrews (13 and up)

*Island of the Blue Dolphins* by Scott O'Dell (12 and up)

*The Moment of Wonder: A Collection of Chinese and Japanese Poetry* edited by Richard Lewis (11 and up)

*Oté: A Puerto Rican Folk Tale* retold by Pura Belpré, ill. by Paul Galdone (7-9)

*Peter and Veronica* by Marilyn Sachs, ill. by Louis Glanzman (10-12)

*The Phantom Tollbooth* by Norton Juster, ill. by Jules Feiffer (9-12)

*The Pigman* by Paul Zindel (12 and up)

*The Snowy Day* written and ill. by Ezra Jack Keats (3-5)

*Sounder* by William H. Armstrong (13 and up)

*Stevie* written and ill. by John Steptoe (5-7)

*Where the Wild Things Are* written and ill. by Maurice Sendak (5-7)

*A Wrinkle in Time* by Madeleine L'Engle (12 and up)

**1970s:**

*Anno's Counting Book* written and ill. by Mitsumasa Anno (3-5)

*The Berenstain Bears' Science Fair* written and ill. by Stan and Jan Berenstain (5-7)

*A Billion for Boris* by Mary Rodgers (10-13)

*Bridge to Terabithia* by Katherine Paterson, ill. by Donna Diamond (10-13)

*The Cat Ate My Gymsuit* by Paula Danziger (12 and up)

*The Chocolate War* by Robert Cormier (12 and up)

*Deenie* by Judy Blume (11-13)

*Dinky Hocker Shoots Smack!* by M. E. Kerr (12 and up)

*Dragonwings* by Lawrence Yep (12 and up)

*El Bronx Remembered* by Nicholasa Mohr (8-12)

*Freight Train* written and ill. by Donald Crew (3-5)

*Frog and Toad Together* written and ill. by Arnold Lobel (5-7)

*George and Martha Encore* written and ill. by James Marshall (5-7)

*The Grey King* by Susan Cooper, ill. by Michael Heslop (11-13)

*Julie of the Wolves* by Jean Craighead George, ill. by John Schoenherr (11 and up)

*M. C. Higgins the Great* by Virginia Hamilton (12-14)

*Mrs. Frisby and the Rats of NIMH* by Robert C. O'Brien, ill. by Zena Bernstein (9-11)

*Noisy Nora* written and ill. by Rosemary Wells (4-7)

*The Owl's Song* by Janet Campbell Hale (12 and up)

*Roll of Thunder, Hear My Cry* by Mildred D. Taylor, ill. by Jerry Pinkney (11-13)

*Sadako and the Thousand Paper Cranes* by Eleanor Coerr, ill. by Ronald Himler (9-12)

*Soup and Me* by Robert Newton Peck, ill. by Charles Lilly (9-11)

*The Stones of Green Knowe* by L. M. Boston, ill. by Peter Boston (10-12)

*Strega Nona* retold and ill. by Tomie de Paola (5-8)

*The Very Hungry Caterpillar* by Eric Carle (3-5)

*Tuck Everlasting* by Natalie Babbitt (10-12)

*Why Mosquitoes Buzz in People's Ears* by Verna Aardema, ill. by Leo and Diane Dillon (7-9)

*William's Doll* by Charlotte Zolotow, ill. William Pène Du Bois (3-5)

## 1980s:

*Commodore Perry in the Land of the Shogun* by Rhoda Blumberg (12 and up)

*Dear Mr. Henshaw* by Beverly Cleary, ill. by Paul O. Zelinsky (8-11)

*Dicey's Song* by Cynthia Voight (12 and up)

*Free Fall* written and ill. by David Wiesner (7-9)

*Hatchet* by Gary Paulsen (11-14)

*How Much Is a Million?* by David Schwartz, ill. by Steven Kellogg (6-8)

*If You Give a Mouse a Cookie* by Laura Joffe Numeroff, ill. by Felicia Bond (3-5)

*In the Year of the Boar and Jackie Robinson* by Bette Bao Lord, ill. by Marc Simont (8 and up)

*The Indian in the Cupboard* by Lynne Reid Banks (9-12)

*Jacob Have I Loved* by Katherine Paterson (13 and up)

*Jumanji* written and ill. by Chris Van Allsburg (7-9)

*Miss Rumphius* written and ill. by Barbara Cooney (7-9)

*The Moon* by Seymour Simon (6-8)

*Mufaro's Beautiful Daughters* written and ill. by John Steptoe (5-8)

*The New Kid on the Block* by Jack Prelutsky, ill. by James Stevenson (8-11)

*Owl Moon* by Jane Yolen, ill. by John Schoenherr (4-6)

*The People Could Fly: American Black Folktales* by Virginia Hamilton, ill. by Leo and Diane Dillon (8 and up)

*Rainbow Jordan* by Alice Childress (12-14)

*Redwall* by Brian Jacques, ill. by Gary Chalk (9-12)

*Sarah, Plain and Tall* by Patricia MacLachlan (9-12)

*Sing a Song of Popcorn: Every Child's Book of Poems* selected by Beatrice Schenk de Regniers and Eva Moore, ill. by Caldecott winners (5-8)

*Stone Fox* by John Reynolds Gardiner, ill. by Marcia Sewall (7-9)

*The Story of Jumping Mouse* retold and ill. by John Steptoe (6-8)

*Ten, Nine, Eight* written and ill. by Molly Bang (3-5)

*Thirteen Ways to Sink a Sub* by Jamie Gilson, ill. by Linda Strauss Edwards (9-11)

*The Whipping Boy* by Sid Fleischman, ill. by Peter Sís (8 and up)


**1990s:**

*The 20th Century Children's Poetry Treasury* selected by Jack Prelutsky, ill. by Meilo So (4-14)

*Abuela* by Arthur Dorros, ill. by Elisa Kleven (6-8)

*Bud, Not Buddy* by Christopher Paul Curtis (9-12)

*Catherine, Called Birdy* by Karen Cushman (10-12)

*Chicka Chicka Boom Boom* by Bill Martin, Jr. and John Archambault, ill. by Lois Ehlert (2-4)

*The Ear, the Eye and the Arm* by Nancy Farmer (12 and up)

*The Golden Compass* by Philip Pullman (12 and up)

*Good Night, Gorilla* written and ill. by Peggy Rathmann (2-4)

*Grandfather's Journey* written and ill. by Allen Say (7-9)

*Guess How Much I Love You* by Sam McBratney, ill. by Anita Jeram (3-5)

*Harry Potter and the Sorcerer's Stone* by J. K. Rowling (10-13)

*Hiroshima* by Laurence Yep (10-14)

*Iqbal Masih and the Crusaders Against Child Slavery* by Susan Kuklin (11-14)

*Joey Pigza Swallowed the Key* by Jack Gantos (9-12)

*Joseph Had a Little Overcoat* written and ill. by Simms Taback (3-5)

*Let's-Read-and-Find-Out Science series: What Makes a Shadow? / Oil Spill* by various authors and illustrators (4-8)

*Lilly' Purple Plastic Purse* written and ill. by Kevin Henkes (5-7)

*A Long Way from Chicago: A Novel in Stories* by Richard Peck (10-13)

*The Magic Schoolbus: Lost in the Solar System* by Joanna Cole, ill. by Bruce Degen (6-10)

*Make Lemonade* by Virginia Euwer Wolff (11-14)

*The Middle Passage: White Ships/ Black Cargo* by Tom Feelings (12 and up)

*My Heroes, My People: African Americans and Native Americans in the West* by Morgan Monceaux and Ruth Katcher, ill. by Morgan Monceaux (7-10)

*Number the Stars* by Lois Lowry (9-12)

*Out of the Dust* by Karen Hesse (11-14)

*Parrot in the Oven: Mi Vida* by Victor Martinez (12-14)

*Pete's A Pizza* written and ill. by William Steig (3-5)

*Shabanu: Daughter of the Wind* by Suzanne Fisher Staples (13 and up)

*Shiloh* by Phyllis Reynolds Naylor (11-14)

*Snowflake Bentley* by Jacqueline Briggs Martin, ill. by Mary Azarian (7-10)

*Tar Beach* written and ill. by Faith Ringgold (5-7)

*Through My Eyes* by Ruby Bridges (7-12)

*Walk Two Moons* by Sharon Creech (11-14)

*Wringer* by Jerry Spinelli (10-12)

## 2000 and beyond:

*The Absolutely True Diary of a Part-Time Indian* by Sherman Alexie, ill. by Ellen Forney (12 and up)

*Always Remember Me: How One Family Survived World War II* written and ill. by Marisabina Russo (9-11)

*The Amazing Maurice and His Educated Rodents* by Terry Pratchett (9-12)

*Amber Was Brave, Essie Was Smart* written and ill. by Vera B. Williams (8-12)

*The Arrival* written and ill. by Shaun Tan (12 and up)

*Brendan Buckley's Universe and Everything in It* by Sundee Tucker Frazier (9-12)

*Carver: A Life In Poems* by Marilyn Nelson (12-14)

*Clementine* by Sara Pennypacker, ill. by Marla Frazee (7-10)

*Click, Clack, Moo: Cows That Type* by Doreen Cronin, ill. by Betsy Lewin (4-8)

*Don't Let the Pigeon Drive the Bus* written and ill. by Mo Willems (4–6)

*Esperanza Rising* by Pam Muñoz Ryan (10–12)

*Here's a Little Poem: A Very First Book of Poetry* collected by Jane Yolen and Andrew Fusek Peters, ill. by Polly Dunbar (3–5)

*How Do Dinosaurs Say Good Night?* by Jane Yolen, ill. by Mark Teague (3–5)

*Ida B. Wells: Mother of the Civil Rights Movement* by Dennis Brindell Fradin and Judith Bloom Fradin (10 and up)

*Kira-Kira* by Cynthia Kadohata (12–14)

*Kitten's First Full Moon* by Kevin Henkes (3–5)

*Koyal Dark, Mango Sweet* by Kashmira Sheth (12–15)

*The Librarian of Basra: A True Story from Iraq* written and ill. by Jeanette Winter (6–9)

*Locomotion* by Jacqueline Woodson (9–12)

*The Man Who Walked Two Towers* written and ill. by Mordicai Gerstein (8–10)

*Moses: When Harriet Tubman Led Her People to Freedom* by Carole Boston Weatherford, ill. by Kadir Nelson (9–12)

*The Poet Slave of Cuba: A Biography of Juan Francisco Manzano* by Margarita Engle, ill. by Sean Qualls (12–14)

*A Single Shard* by Linda Sue Park (9–12)

*Something Remains* by Inge Barth-Grözinger, trans. by Anthea Bell (12–14)

*The Stray Dog* retold and ill. by Marc Simont (3–5)

*The Tale of Despereaux* by Kate DiCamillo, ill. by Timothy Basil Ering (8–11)

*This Land Was Made for You and Me: The Life and Songs of Woody Guthrie* by Elizabeth Partridge (12–14)

*Who Was First? Discovering the Americas* by Russell Freedman (10–14)

# AWARD BOOKS: 1943–2008

## Key
(JF) – Josette Frank Award
(CL) – Claudia Lewis Award
(FSS) – Flora Stieglitz Straus Award
(LA) – Lifetime Achievement Award

## 2008

*Home of the Brave*
by Katherine Applegate
Feiwel & Friends (JF)

*Here's a Little Poem*
collected by Jane Yolen and Andrew Fusek Peters, ill. by Polly Dunbar
Candlewick Press (CL)

*This Is Just to Say: Poems of Apology and Forgiveness*
by Joyce Sidman, ill. by Pamela Zagarenski
Houghton Mifflin (CL)

*Ballerina Dreams*
by Lauren Thompson, photos by James Estrin
Feiwel & Friends (FSS)

*Who Was First? Discovering the Americas*
by Russell Freedman
Clarion (FSS)

## 2007

*Clementine*
by Sara Pennypacker, ill. by Marla Frazee
Hyperion (JF)

*The Manny Files*
by Christian Burch
Atheneum (JF)

*Freedom Walkers*
by Russell Freedman
Holiday House (FSS)

## 2006

*Each Little Bird That Sings*
by Deborah Wiles
Harcourt (JF)

*A Kick in the Head*
selected by Paul B. Janeczko, ill. by Chris Raschka
Candlewick Press (CL)

*Gorilla Doctors*
by Pamela S. Turner
Houghton Mifflin (FSS)

## 2005

*Ida B*
by Katherine Hannigan
Greenwillow (JF)

*Here in Harlem*
by Walter Dean Myers
Holiday (CL)

*Hummingbird Nest*
by Kristine O'Connell George
Harcourt (CL)

*The Librarian of Basra*
by Jeanette Winter
Harcourt (FSS)

*The Race to Save the Lord God Bird*
by Phillip Hoose
FSG (FSS)

## 2004

*The Goose Girl*
by Shannon Hale
Bloomsbury (JF)

*The Way a Door Closes*
by Hope Anita Smith
Henry Holt (CL)

*Yesterday I Had the Blues*
by Jeron Ashford Frame
Tricycle (CL)

*Hana's Suitcase*
by Karen Levine
Albert Whitman (FSS)

*Moon, Have You Met My Mother?*
by Karla Kuskin
HarperCollins (LA)

## 2003

*Goddess of Yesterday*
by Caroline B. Cooney
Delacorte (JF)

*Jericho Walls*
by Kristi Collier
Henry Holt (JF)

*Little Dog and Duncan*
by Kristine O'Connell George, ill. by June Otani
Clarion (CL)

*No More!*
by Doreen Rappaport, ill. by Shane W. Evans
Candlewick (FSS)

*When Marian Sang*
by Pam Muñoz Ryan, ill. by Brian Selznick
Scholastic (FSS)

## 2002

*Amber Was Brave, Essie Was Smart*
by Vera B. Williams
Greenwillow (JF and CL)

*Love That Dog*
by Sharon Creech
HarperCollins (CL)

*Carver*
by Marilyn Nelson
Front Street (FSS)

**2001**

*Because of Winn-Dixie*
by Kate DiCamillo
Candlewick (JF)

*Mammalabilia*
by Douglas Florian
Harcourt (CL)

*Ida B. Wells*
by Dennis Brindell Fradin
and Judith Bloom Fradin
Clarion (FSS)

**2000**

*Figuring Out Frances*
by Gina Willner-Pardo
Clarion (JF)

*Stop Pretending*
by Sonya Sones
HarperCollins (CL)

*Through My Eyes*
by Ruby Bridges
Scholastic (FSS)

**1999***

**1998**

*My Louisiana Sky*
by Kimberly Willis Holt
Henry Holt (JF)

*I, Too, Sing America*
by Catherine Clinton
Houghton Mifflin (CL)

*Iqbal Masih and the
Crusaders Against Child
Slavery*
by Susan Kuklin
Henry Holt (FSS)

**1997**

*No Turning Back*
by Beverley Naidoo
HarperCollins

*Wringer*
by Jerry Spinelli
HarperCollins (JF)

*The Invisible Ladder*
Edited by Liz Rosenberg
Holt (CL)

*Oh, Freedom!*
by Casey King and Linda
Barrett Osborne
Knopf (FSS)

**1996**

*The Cuckoo's Child*
by Suzanne Freeman
Greenwillow

**1995**

*Music from a Place
Called Half Moon*
by Jerrie Oughton
Houghton Mifflin

*The Watsons Go to
Birmingham—1963*
by Christopher Paul Curtis
Delacorte

*Parallel Journeys*
by Eleanor Ayer
Atheneum (FSS)

**1994**

*Earthshine*
by Theresa Nelson
Orchard

**1993**

*Make Lemonade*
by Virginia Euwer Wolff
Henry Holt & Co.

*Eleanor Roosevelt:
A Life of Discovery*
by Russell Freedman
Clarion Books (FSS)

**1992**

*Blue Skin of the Sea*
by Graham Salisbury
Delacorte

**1991**

*Shadow Boy*
by Susan E. Kirby
Orchard

**1990**

*Secret City, U.S.A.*
by Felice Holman
Scribner's

**1989**

*Shades of Gray*
by Carolyn Reeder
Macmillan

**1988**

*The Most Beautiful Place
in the World*
by Ann Cameron
Knopf

*December Stillness*
by Mary Downing Hahn
Clarion

**1987**

*Rabble Starkey*
by Lois Lowry
Houghton Mifflin

**1986**

*Journey to Jo'burg*
by Beverley Naidoo
Lippincott

**1985**

*With Westie and the Tin Man*
by C. S. Adler
Macmillan

*Ain't Gonna Study War
No More*
by Milton Meltzer
Harper & Row
(Special Citation)

**1984**

*One-Eyed Cat*
by Paula Fox
Bradbury

---

*After 1999, the awards were presented in the year
following the copyright date of the book.

## 1983

*The Sign of the Beaver*
by Elizabeth George Speare
Houghton Mifflin

*The Solomon System*
by Phyllis Reynolds Naylor
Atheneum

## 1982

*Homesick: My Own Story*
by Jean Fritz
Putnam

## 1981

*A Spirit to Ride the
Whirlwind*
by Athena Lord
Macmillan

## 1980

*A Boat to Nowhere*
by Maureen C. Wartski
Westminster

## 1979

*The Whipman Is Watching*
by T. A. Dyer
Houghton Mifflin

## 1978

*The Devil in Vienna*
by Doris Orgel
Dial

## 1977

*The Pinballs*
by Betsy Byars
Harper

## 1976

*Somebody Else's Child*
by Roberta Silman
Warne

## 1975

*The Garden Is Doing Fine*
by Carol Farley
Atheneum

## 1974

*Luke Was There*
by Eleanor Clymer
Holt, Rinehart & Winston

## 1973

*A Taste of Blackberries*
by Doris Buchanan Smith
T. Y. Crowell

## 1972

*A Sound of Chariots*
by Mollie Hunter
Harper

## 1971

*John Henry McCoy*
by Lillie D. Chafin
Macmillan

*The Pair of Shoes*
by Aline Glasgow
Dial (Special Citation)

## 1970

*Rock Star*
by James Lincoln Collier
Four Winds

*Migrant Girl*
by Carli Laklan
McGraw-Hill

## 1969

*The Empty Moat*
by Margaretha Shemin
Coward-McCann

## 1968

*What It's All About*
by Vadim Frolov
Doubleday

*Where Is Daddy?
The Story About Divorce*
by Beth Goff
Beacon (Special Citation)

## 1967

*The Contender*
by Robert Lipsyte
Harper

## 1966

*Queenie Peavy*
by Robert Burch
Viking

*Curious George Goes
to the Hospital*
by Margaret and H. A. Rey
Houghton Mifflin
(Special Citation)

## 1965

*The Empty Schoolhouse*
by Natalie Savage Carlson
Harper

## 1964

*The High Pasture*
by Ruth Harnden
Houghton Mifflin

## 1963

*The Peaceable Revolution*
by Betty Schechter
Houghton Mifflin

*The Rock and the Willow*
by Mildred Lee
Lothrop, Lee & Shepard

## 1962

*The Trouble with Terry*
by Joan Lexau
Dial

## 1961

*The Road to Agra*
by Aimee Sommerfelt
Criterion

*The Girl from Puerto Rico*
by Hila Colman
Morrow

## 1960

*Janine*
by Robin McKown
Messner

## 1959

*Jennifer*
by Zoa Sherburne
Morrow

## 1958

*South Town*
by Lorenze Graham
Follett

## 1957

*Shadow Across the Campus*
by Helen R. Sattley
Dodd, Mead

## 1956

*The House of Sixty Fathers*
by Meindert de Jong
Harper

## 1955

*Plain Girl*
by Virginia Sorenson
Harcourt, Brace & World

*Crow Boy*
by Taro Yashima
Viking

## 1954

*The Ordeal of the
Young Hunter*
by Jonreed Lauritzen
Little, Brown

*High Road Home*
by William Corbin
Coward-McCann

## 1953

*In a Mirror*
by Mary Stolz
Harper

## 1952

*Jareb*
by Miriam Powell
T. Y. Crowell

*Twenty and Ten*
by Claire Huchet Bishop
Viking

## 1951

No Award

## 1950

*Partners*
by Eleanor Roosevelt &
Helen Ferris
Doubleday

## 1949

*Paul Tiber*
by Marie Gleit
Scribner

## 1948

*The Big Wave*
by Pearl Buck
John Day

## 1947

*Judy's Journey*
by Lois Lenski
Lippincott

## 1946

*Heart of Danger*
by Howard Pease
Doubleday

## 1945

*The Moved-Outers*
by Florence Cranell Means
Houghton Mifflin

## 1944

*The House*
by Margorie Hill Alee
Houghton Mifflin

## 1943

*Keystone Kids*
by John R. Tunis
Harcourt, Brace & World

# THE CHILDREN'S BOOK COMMITTEE

# PUBLISHERS

Abrams
Aladdin
Albert Whitman
Amistad
Amulet
Arthur A. Levine
Athenuem
August House
Bearport
Bloomsbury
Blue Sky
Boyds Mills
Calkins Creek
Candlewick
Carolrhoda
Cavendish
Charlesbridge
Chicken House
Children's Book
Child's Play
Chronicle
Cinco Puntos
Clarion
Compass Point
David Fickling
Delacorte
Dial
DK
Dutton
Eerdmans
Enchanted Lion
Farrar Straus Giroux
Feiwel & Friends
Fitzhenry & Whiteside
Franklin Mason Press
Front Street
Gibbs Smith
Global Content Ventures
Grosset
Harcourt
HarperCollins
Henry Holt
Holiday House
Houghton Mifflin
Hyperion

Jump at the Sun
Kane/Miller
Kar-Ben
Kids Can
Kingfisher
Knopf
Lee & Low
Lemniscaat
Lerner
Little Brown
Little Simon
McElderry
Millbrook
National Geographic
Orca
Orchard
Peachtree
Penguin
Philomel
Picture Window
Putnam
Random
Raven Productions
razOrbill

Red Deer Press
Roaring Brook
Scholastic
Schwartz & Wade
Second Story
Simon & Schuster
Sleeping Bear
Smithsonian
Sourcebooks
Speak
St. Martin's
Sterling Publications
Sylvan Dell
Toon Books
Tradewind Books
Tricycle
Tundra
Twenty-First Century
Viking
Walker
Wayne State University
Wendy Lamb
Wish Publishing
Wordsong

## ILLUSTRATIONS BY

Amy Wummer © 2008 by Amy Wummer from *Chess: I Love It! I Love It!* by Jamie Gilson. Reprinted by permission of Clarion Books, an imprint of Houghton Mifflin Harcourt Publishing Company.

Marla Frazee © 2008 by Marla Frazee from *Clementine's Letter* by Sara Pennypacker. Reprinted by permission of the artist.

Nick Bruel © 2008 by Nick Bruel from *Clever Duck* by Dick King-Smith. Reprinted by permission of Henry Holt and Company, LLC.

Peter Bailey © 2007 by Peter Bailey from *Ibby's Magic Weekend* by Heather Dyer. Reprinted by permission of The Chicken House.

Harry Horse © 1998 by Harry Horse from *The Last Gold Diggers*. Reprinted by permission of Peachtree Publishers.

James Stevenson © 2008 by James Stevenson from *My Dog May Be a Genius* by Jack Prelutsky. Reprinted by permission of HarperCollins Publishers.

# INDEX

# THE BANK STREET CENTER
# FOR CHILDREN'S LITERATURE

**The Bank Street Center for Children's Literature** aims to reverse a growing trend: the diminishing use of children's literature in literacy programs and the increase in dull materials that stress rote and repetition. The result is that many children now find it difficult to "engage" in their own learning. Engaging children in literature and learning is what the Center is all about. **Learning to read** merely gives a child a tool for acquiring information. **Loving to read** equips a child with a whole set of tools for developing a rich, imaginative, and fully experienced life. Our goal is to restore children's literature to its central place in children's learning by fostering, in parents, educators, and especially policy makers, a commitment to and an understanding of the principle that good literature is fundamental to children's learning and social-emotional and aesthetic development.

**The Children's Book Committee** is one of three long-standing Bank Street institutions affiliated with the Bank Street Center for Children's Literature.

The Center's other two affiliates are:

**The Bank Street Writers Lab,** established in 1937 by Bank Street founder, Lucy Sprague Mitchell, provides a supportive workshop for children's book authors. Initial members included Margaret Wise Brown, Ruth Krauss, Claudia Lewis, Clement Hurd, Irma Simonton Black, and later, Maurice Sendak. In the 1960s, many members worked on the groundbreaking *Bank Street Readers,* the first to feature multi-ethnic urban children. Over the years, members and former members have continued to win many awards and accolades, including Newbery and Caldecott awards.

**The Irma S. and James H. Black Picture Book Award,** created in 1972 to honor Irma Simonton Black, a founding member of the Writers Lab, children's book author, and head of Bank Street's Publications Division, now honors her husband as well. It is given each year to an excellent new book for young children that embodies a seamless synthesis of text and illustration. Children themselves make the final choice of the winner and the two to three runners-up. Classes in 13 schools participate in special reading and discussion programs before voting. Maurice Sendak, Irma's close friend, designed the seal for the award.

The Children's Book Committee
Bank Street College of Education
610 West 112th Street
New York, NY 10025
212/875-4540
fax 212/875-4759
e-mail: bookcom@bankstreet.edu
website: www.bankstreet.edu/bookcom/